PRAISE FC
INSIDE PELE'S CHAOS...

Below are testimonials gathered from amongst hundreds of responses to essays previously posted on social media, all of which have been included in this book. It was largely in response to readers' encouragement and requests for more that this book was born.

Mahalo nui loa

You really have a way with story-telling, makes it personal. And you are correct about how we deal with this loss. Many people, though they can hide it well, are emotionally scarred from this event. I saw it in my friends' eyes, hell – I see it in the mirror some nights. Appreciate you taking the time to write this.

~ Dane DuPont

Aloha mahalo nui loa, Beautiful brave warrior gypsy soul. I am deeply thankful for your openness. I feel every ounce of your love and your pain. Your connection, your feeling lost, and also found. I don't feel like I can possibly offer you anything other than my love and aloha.

~ Ayres Vanessa Root

Only a few people in this world are blessed and ready and connected enough to be able to experience what you did and still do. And you are now gifting us with being able to put this energy into words. You seem like a very special being, dear. And the few real ones I met also experienced incredible darkness, countless dark nights of the soul. I think most of us humans live in the in-between most of the time and try to make the best of it. You, dear one were graced to feel HOME, the place we all yearn for. It's a spiritual place, a place of grace, of feeling healed, loved and whole. Will you find it again in form of land? Or will it be found within and expressed through your gift of words and storytelling? I wish I knew and could tell you, sweet love.

~ Alessandra Rupar-Weber

I just read [one of} your [essays] AGAIN. And I could hardly see through my tears.. it is one of the most incredible and profound [essays] I've ever come across. It hits me right where I live. Right in the gut. I can't love it any more. It's literally giving me so much life. I just wanted to add, my deepest most heart full sympathies for your loss. I am feeling deeply blessed and grateful my friend brought this to my attention today. I can't thank you enough for sharing. Mahalo nui loa, aloha ke akua.

~ Ayres Vanessa Root

Wow that was deep and intense. Never do I sit and read long paragraphs of anything, but this time I stopped, listened, and read. You reached into my heart and mind and made me look in the mirror.

~ Martin M. MonDragon

Wow, just wow! You brought me to tears. Your raw emotion touches my soul. Thank you for sharing.

~ Kristie Simpson .

Your words are beautiful and stirring and profound and opening.

~ Marcella McMahon

Ka Uhane ha'a ha'a mai'ola mai, mahalo ia oe ...Kumu Leina'ala...."Audis"...

~ Audis Brown-Dombrigues

Your insights reflect and help people understand grief, whether it's the loss of a home or in my case a husband. Thank you for this beautiful reminder to treat all people gently; we don't know what grief they may be living through.

~ Jan Makinson Ferree

You have given a voice to many many people today who are grieving, no matter what it is they are grieving.... you truly gave a gift of validation and respect to so many going through this process.

~ Sarah Chaput

God, that was well written!!!! Thank you! I'm not someone in Hawaii who has lost things to lava, but I AM someone who, just in life, has lost things, had things taken away, given away things. Your words gave life to my feelings.

~ Kendra Hankins Morton

INSIDE PELE'S CHAOS:
Eruptions in the Rainforest

A memoir of the Kilauea eruptions
in Hawaii in 2018

by
Corey Hale

Publisher's Disclaimer: The author assumes all responsibility for the
accuracy of the content within, as well as liability for permissions.

ISBN: 978-1-950186-14-3

Cover photo of Pāhoa Village
by Faith LeLievre
www.faithlelievrephotography.com

Cover and interior design by Jennifer Leigh Selig
www.jenniferleighselig.com

MANDORLA BOOKS
WWW.MANDORLABOOKS.COM

DEDICATION

To my Gram.

And to all the wanderers who are not lost.

. . .

From the Heart of a Wander Woman

I know the way I live unsettles you.
But I'm not unsettled.
I'm a traveler, a Wander Woman.

I'm not looking for everlasting four walls,
or the right man, or outer peace.

I am my home, and four walls would hem me in.
I am at peace when I accept that
THIS is my true nature.

What I'm looking for is intangible and fantastical.

Please don't wish for me to find
what would make you happy.
I love you, but know
that such a wish being fulfilled
would be for your comfort,
and not for mine.

If you have wishes to spare,
and want to gift one to me,
wish for clear vision,
serendipitous connections,
and soft landings.

TABLE OF CONTENTS

INTRODUCTION

You must have chaos within you to give birth to a dancing star.
~Friedrich Nietzsche

This is a kind of backwards and forwards book. Most of the essays are dated, but many are out of order. This is not to confuse you, but to allow for your own interpretations, and to show how pieces of the story were talking to each other before they happened.

We know how this ends, with lava and loss, which adds to the eeriness of the foreshadowing. I wrote what I wrote, in the moment, while a hand greater than mine hinted at the future.

I revere Pele, and she has honored me by being a presence in my life. To be Inside Pele's Chaos was to experience firsthand what was breathtaking and devastating and surreal.

Possibilities we'd never have otherwise considered were thrust upon us by the shifting landscape. The challenge being to find the form in the chaos instead of trying to fit the chaos into someone else's form.

We had no control.

Chaos is more than destruction, more than a mess without purpose. Chaos is where everything exists at once, where creation begins. We got to be a part of this most sacred of events, as Pele gave birth to more world.

Chaos is where all great dreams begin.

Woman in the Sky

I saw her over 20 years ago. She filled the sky - pointing toward the island of Hawaii.

In 1997, on one of my return trips to Maui, I went camping in Hana. There's an open, grassy field where you can choose to camp under the trees or under the stars, all next to what feels like the edge of the world and the ever-glorious tropical sunrises and moonsets.

On this night, in this place with no light pollution, and an absent moon, the sky was filled with billions and billions of stars. It was so bright I was writing by starlight...then I lay back to gaze and my eyes were filled with a vision of *a woman in petroglyph form who filled the entire sky. She was an ancient feminine outline created by stars, held by a deep velvet of black so dark that it was blue. I looked away to see if it was my imagination. But she was there. She stayed there, one arm on her spiral hip and the other pointed east, toward the Big Island, the island of Hawaii.*

I doodled this image throughout graduate school. I carved her into my pottery, embossed her on my checks, and silk-screened her onto fundraising t-shirts. When anyone asked who she was, and what she was pointing toward, I said I didn't know.

But I did know, it was Pele, and I knew she was telling me to go to the Big Island. I wasn't ready to go though, so I wouldn't speak the words. As soon as I said them, I knew it would be time to go.

It took me twenty years to get here. It was she who brought me to Puna, she who brought me to my land, and it was she who protected me all the years I lived in my jungle, alone, with my cat, and for a while, my puppy.

I knew I was home when I looked down on my land from above and saw her form in the three craters lined up behind me.

12/4/18

Seeing the similarities of the craters behind my land to the Woman in the Sky.

I've been writing this book in my head every day, all day, for as long as I can remember. Always waiting for that magical day of true inspiration. The day when it's easy. The day when it pours out of me effortlessly. Where the form and the structure don't struggle for dominance over the story. Where what I have to say, and how I say it is a rallying call for hope.

I'm trying to be a certain way. Trying to be an objective author. An evolved human. A strong person.

Someone with the answers to the catastrophes. The epiphanies to the disasters. Someone to inspire. To admire. Someone who's been through the fire. Someone who is FINE.

Useless. Pointless. My story may be one of success simply because I survived to begin again.

Is this about my history, or about the lava?

Yes.

My life is barely there. Surviving the lava didn't bring me robust health. It didn't heal family rifts. Quite the opposite. Their decisions during that time were the final nails in the coffin of our relational demise.

I'm not sad about this. It's a relief for it to finally be over.

To write only about the lava would be incomplete. I can't leave out my history. But I also don't need to include it all. This isn't about my childhood, or about my absent relatives, or about my son. But the eruptions also didn't happen in a vacuum, and they healed me in these areas in ways I didn't expect.

Who we are, and how we cope is informed by where we come from. Someday I'll write more about the dysfunctional family part of my life.

Who am I writing for? Me, you, those who came before or after? Is this something I have to know, or is it enough to say I write for those who've been struck silent?

The lava made us raw. It pierced us in primal places. It brought out the best in some, and in others it brought out the ugly. So, while I reference my family history, this isn't about them. It's about me and you, and it's about Puna.

It's about how a natural disaster can snap you to attention and shift your priorities in ways that nothing else can, because our lives run parallel to metaphors and allegories. And natural disasters are full of them. Sometimes they are obvious, like my 'randomly' choosing to fly to Phoenix, after having my life reduced to ashes by the lava.

Usually they're more subtle though, and we brush them off as mere coincidences. Except, there are no coincidences, only synchronicities.

So, I write, knowing that I'm afraid of this journey, and of what I might find as I revisit the exhilaration and the trauma of what we experienced. The ground beneath us and inside of us, shook and cracked and spewed forth fire. In that fire were our demons, our angels, our mentors, and our fears.

One year ago, on December 5th, 2018, Kilauea was downgraded to normal, after more than 30 years of eruptions. The 13 acres that the 2018 eruptions covered or created, continues to cool and crumble, and steam still rises in many areas and isn't likely to ever stop. There are green ferns appearing in cracks on the barren landscape, and new roads are being bulldozed so people can go home. Even if home has been reduced from abundant jungle to crumbling lava. It's still home.

Our lava disaster created an intimacy and an urgency that allowed our walls to collapse for a period. Because we had a common purpose. A reason to come together. To rely on, and to take care of one another.

Then it was over. And that sense of purpose along with it. And I don't know how to continue to know you in that intimate way, or to believe you'll stick around. I'm not your job. I don't want to be your burden.

I am strong. Strong enough to take care of myself. To not need. To know how to love, but not too deeply.

There's another kind of strength I'm less familiar with. It involves the kind of love that means it hurts to be apart. It's why my love for Lily, and my land, my gypsy wagon, my life, and the pond broke my heart.

I knew I could love them deeply and they wouldn't hurt me. They would never leave me.

But then the planet took it to a whole new level. Took from me what I'd sunk my heart into (my love). And I feel embarrassed to have been caught at being so openly betrayed. To have shown how much I loved and how much I lost. I dared to love a Place and it left me. Alone. Completely.

I despise these words and this transparency with you. Because I know they are lies I tell myself. I know nothing left me. That it, none of it, was personal. That I'm not alone. I know there is no better way to unravel a belief system than to reveal it. Unveil it for the fiction that it is.

I'm not a victim.

The universe hasn't chosen me specifically for anything. This is not the story of Job.

I'm not unique. Not in that way.

The truth is, this really is a conspiracy.

Not a conspiracy to keep us down. But a conspiracy to give us every opportunity to resolve a litany of beliefs that are no longer useful. We must unravel what we think is true, because what's true is, what we believe in the moment is just the next thing to know on the way to knowing what we're going to know next.

My concern about writing objectively is about confronting one truth, which is, I cannot control what you get from what I write. I can't make you understand. I can't stop you from thinking that I'm fucked up, any more than I can stop you from being inspired.

What I can do, is tell the truth when I'd rather not, and even, or especially, when I think it might destroy what you think of me.

It takes courage for us to tell each other the stupid things our brain tells us are true. The stupid ways in which it tries to take us out. It's easier to cower behind the wise words we once read in a book, and put on a good face, pretending to be something we aren't. Even to ourselves. Mostly to ourselves.

We don't lie to each other on purpose. We believe what we say because we believe what we think. Because we believe what we read. And because we read it, we think we are it. But we aren't. We are on our way though.

Refusing to question what we think causes us to be less authentic. Less able to become more. Who we're supposed to be isn't always who we actually are.

This is our shadow. No one is immune.

The more we tell on ourselves, the less we have to fear being found out. It's part of the human condition.

In that way, I am a success. I'm willing to risk appearing the fool, only knowing what I know until I know something else.

As my book becomes more real, as I invest more heavily in myself and its success. I find myself waking up thinking about how stupid the whole thing is, and that I should just quit.

Which finally clued me in to what's going on. My fear of letting go of obscurity.

Mediocrity. Anonymity.

Someone asked me a few years ago why I didn't write my book. I said because I'm afraid I'll be killed. They asked me why, what the heck was I going to write?

It doesn't matter. There will always be someone who doesn't approve. That's not the point. And maybe I will be killed. Or maybe parts of my ego will be left behind that no longer serve me. Or maybe I was killed in a past lifetime for saying what was on my mind.

Or maybe it's something else. None of it matters because it's all in the perception. If I think it's true, then it is. It's important to proceed with caution when we're thinking.

We carry around the strangest ideas in our heads.

I've never had a plan, just a really long bucket list.

HOW TO READ THIS BOOK

This is a kind of hybrid book that reflects the way that we read and gather information in the digital age. If you're holding a paper copy, you'll want to make note of my webpage [www.coreyhale.com] so you can enjoy the interactive nature between the hi- and lo-tech experience. If you're reading the e-book version, you'll find links throughout that will take you directly to my resources webpage, where you'll find timelines, photo essays, links to other people's videos, and my newspaper interviews.

I've also included excerpts from my Facebook video live feeds. The live feeds were my way of documenting and staying connected to the outside world during a time when I found it difficult to write. They are raw, and they are real, and you can watch them, as well as read the transcripts in their entirety at the links provided throughout, or go to www.coreyhale.com and go to the Resources page.

I knew when the eruptions began that I would write about them. Because of the overwhelming nature of the experience, I wasn't able to keep strict journals or notes. I couldn't write and I couldn't talk on the phone, it was too much to process. My live feeds served the purpose of keeping my friends and family informed (the news was doing such a poor job of it) and allowed me to keep track of what was happening so I could look back at a later time.

That time is now.

Some of the live feeds are heartbreaking. and I don't look pretty, all of which reflects the progression of events. In the beginning, I'm ragged, and as we settle into the flow — literally — it shows in how I show up. It's not a linear journey, this, but an ebb and flow (there's that metaphor) and how we rode the waves as individuals and as a community.

There are also some Hawaiian words, which you'll find more completely explained in the glossary on my website.[1] While I don't speak the language fluently, many Hawaiian words are part of our daily conversation. It's fitting that they be used here.

There is a storyline, and you're free to read from front to back. You can also choose to skip around. Visit the website where I've created photo essays for you, of my land, the pond, flow maps, and the evolution of the evacuation center parking lot. This experience was intense to live through, and equally as intense to write about. Many things happened and were condensed into a short period of time. Too short to properly process while they were happening. This is reflected in the essays, and at times this might be overwhelming. I know it was for me. I suggest you do what I did while writing. Take time to walk away. Sit in the sun. Have a glass of wine or cup of tea. Do something that makes your dog's tail wag or your cat purr. Let it settle in. And don't worry, I promise that in the end it's all okay.

GRATITUDE AND RECOGNITION

I offer my gratitude to my hanai brothers and sisters, and my ohana in Puna and around the world. My love to you for being on this journey with me.

It's also important that I acknowledge the health conditions that heavily influenced my decisions. Without the chronic fatigue and pain, I'd never have held still long enough to consider buying land, I'd have been off and running across the planet when I got my settlement check. Without my health holding me in place, I'd have found ways to NOT face the things I finally have.

Thank you to my team. To Allie Smith, my patient taskmaster, and brilliant editor, Jennifer Leigh Selig, my equally brilliant publisher, and to Francesca Ripple who worked during her vacation to complete my website.

It's my honor to bring this book into the world. May it be as healing for you in the reading, as it has been for me in the writing.

---

[1] www.coreyhale.com/gallery

Depth, Eco, Archetype

I see the world around me, and the things in it, as conscious, living beings. You might say this is you too, or you might say that this is one crazy woman and I'm outta here. By the end of this book, you also might see the world outside your window differently. You may realize that some of the things you imagined were real.

I was born a psychologist, if by psychologist you mean an observer of human behavior. And I was born to be a Depth Psychologist, which means it's not just the behavior that intrigues me, but what's beneath it, what drives it.

Inside of Depth Psychology, I found two other treasure — Archetypal Psychology, the study of myth and things of mythical proportions, and Ecopsychology, which places us back in alignment with the consciousness of the World.

Places have experiences that affect the way they exist. Their history influences them in the same ways ours does us. There is no way, within the space of a few pages of an essay, that I can describe and explain all the things there are to know of Depth, or Eco, or Archetypal Psychology. But these are the tunes that play in my life. They are the reason that I will capitalize a word, like Place or Fire, in the middle of a sentence. Because I'm speaking of them in a larger sense of the word. Not as a fire in the fireplace, but as the Fire that plays an active role in a moment, or in an event. When the lava is erupting, the Lava is changing how we think of things.

> *How strange that the nature of life is change, yet the nature of human beings is to resist change. And how ironic that the difficult times we fear might ruin us are the very ones that can break us open and help us become who we were meant to be.*

PROLOGUE

7/22/18

After evacuation, I was able to go home once. It was brief because while I was there fissure 7 happened. I got a text message from one of the automated alerts systems I was on, probably Civil Defense, saying, "Get out now." After that day, there were continuous streaming poisonous clouds of SO2 (vog) that would keep me from ever going in again.

While I was there, I was able to grab a half-dozen boxes. Boxes I brought from the mainland a few years ago and had stored on and beneath my jungle platform. They were waiting for my bigger home to be built. I didn't know what was in the boxes I was able to reach. I just grabbed. I was scared. It felt weird and dangerous. The air smelled like Kool-Aid, which I didn't understand, and my eyes burned from the chemicals and smoke.

I couldn't reach the boxes I wanted, the ones with pictures and the ones with mine and my son's Christmas decorations.

I couldn't find my great-grandfather's ship's compass and sextant.

I stood there watching my trees die, dry leaves fluttering to the ground like rain. I heard the helicopters overhead and the roaring of the lava over the hill. And still, I thought, *this is silly, the fissures are going toward the ocean now, they've passed me. I'll be back here in a few days and this will have been for no good reason.*

Since that day, I've barely glanced inside the boxes. If I don't look too closely, I can't say for sure what is gone. When I opened one of them all the way, I found my yearbooks and one of Sean's favorite childhood books, *There's a Monster in my Lunchbox.* I found a few new Christmas ornaments I'd bought for Sean that hadn't made it into the Christmas box. I found some seashells, a few tiny treasures, a dozen pictures in a baggie, and a couple of papers that I wrote in graduate school.

It gave me a headache. I don't know when I'll go through the next box. It's a strange feeling, opening mystery boxes. Afraid I'll find something meaningless and equally afraid of finding crazy little things that matter.

It's only when we learn to recognize the beauty
in fragmentation that we transcend. That we evolve.

1/20/19

We stopped at the Y of Pohoiki Road and the road to Kapoho. We went as far as we could in both directions which isn't very far. I took some pictures by moonlight. It was a spur of the moment decision. No time to think of whether we were ready or not, we just went.

It was a good idea. We were alone. It was quiet. Hardly any coquis, especially compared to how loud it once was.

I'm sure it'll be a different experience in the daylight but not so fraught with anticipation as it might have been had we not done this spontaneously.

The one thing I wanted to do during the flow was to be right at this exact spot, the closest I could come to being connected to my place. I'd cry to think of it.

But last night, finally standing there, I was okay. Blank. It was peaceful.

Maybe it'll be that way when I go home. First, I must find a way to get there.

SECTION ONE:
HAWAII

CHAPTER 1:
I'm Buying Land

8/12/15

I'm buying land.

In all beginnings are endings, in all endings are beginnings.

I'm buying land to live on, in a tent and on a platform for now. In my imagination, I see my friends sitting in and around it laughing, creating, and figuring out the ways in which we'll bring other dreams of dreams to life in the coming years.

To date, the most expensive thing I've purchased was my truck. I've never owned land. Or a house. Ever. I've never wanted to.

Why?

Because being tied to one place by such things has been too high a price for this Wander Woman to pay.

I knew this when I was 21 and living in the San Francisco Bay Area, in a two-bedroom apartment. I had a pool. I was a block from Pickleweed Park on the edge of San Francisco Bay. My place was fully furnished with the many (too many) antiques I'd collected growing up in a family of collectors. I had LOTS of stuff—perfume bottles, champagne glasses, gravy boats, storybook dolls, and first-edition books. I had an 18-place setting of Depression Era glassware; my pattern was Petalware. I had 150+ Hull pottery vases. I had an incredibly uncomfortable, albeit beautiful couch from the 1800s. I had china cabinets and oak tables and I had black and white movie photos on my walls.

And I realized...I was possessed by my possessions.

That my plants would die if I went away for even a week.

That my stuff would get lonely without me. I felt obligated to be there to keep it company.

I bit the bullet and sold it. My family was appalled. They'd always said it was an investment I could sell if I needed to, but they meant in some far distant future under dire circumstances. Certainly not now, and definitely not just to travel.

I kept a few things, but over the years I learned to only keep my treasures.

Which is how my travels began.

I've lived on sailboats, in RVs, in convents and monasteries, and lots of places in between. I've driven across the US three or four, five, maybe seven times.

I've accumulated more households of stuff in all these moves and divested myself of that stuff just as many times. I used to sell it. Now I give it away. Twice I've cherry-picked my treasures and walked away from the rest, inviting my neighbors to come in and help themselves. There's so much furniture in the world that when I need more, it finds me. It always finds me.

But I have my boxes. They are my treasure boxes. Items I've gathered in my travels, or heirlooms passed down from my grandparents and great grandparents.

I have only one collection, instead of the dozen I had growing up, and those are my glass fishing floats.

The glass floats that survived.

Over 100 glass fishing floats that range in size from one inch across, to 18 or 20 inches across and come in varied colors and shapes. What they have in common is they begin their journey tied in neat little rows to fishing nets out in the deepest parts of the ocean. The currents and sun and saltwater erode the line holding them to the nets, causing one or two, or an entire length to eventually break off, releasing them to float off on the waves. On to their next adventure.

After a while, they get caught in a giant loop current, called the North Pacific drift, that runs off the coast of Japan, Alaska, the West Coast, and Mexico. An enormous glittering necklace of glass floats bobbing along, traveling thousands of miles, around and around and around.

Until there is a storm.

Then, from this floating chain of sparkling floats that have lived their lives floating around the ocean, the storm plucks a few, tossing them up onto the nearest shoreline.

Which is how I feel right now. As if I've been free-floating in a current that took me from here to there and back again. But that's all about to change.

Because.

I'm buying land. Me. Land. In Hawaii!!! I'm casting myself onto this shore and here is where my new life begins.

I'm going to build platforms for my glamping tents. And have marble-tiled, outdoor showers. And avocado trees. And banana and papaya. And wheelbarrows and tools. I'm going to hang my glass floats from the trees where they will catch the sunlight. There will be rainbows.

My heart has belonged to Hawaii since I was 17 when I first visited the island of Oahu. Waikiki didn't impress me, too many people, but my three weeks on the North Shore, which at that time had only two condo/hotels, stole my heart. I knew I'd be back.

I've returned many times since, and over the years have lived or worked on all the islands, except for the Big Island. I saved it. I knew that someday I'd make my final return, and I'd come here. It's bigger than all the other islands combined and has secrets I haven't yet discovered. It also feels a lot like the North Shore on Oahu from back in the day, and Pahoa Village, with its old storefronts and eccentric free spirits, reminds me of Lahaina in the eighties.

Last December, the day to come back to stay arrived. I was at my Dad's. I was holding my cat, Lily, as I walked down the outside stairs and my knee gave out. I cushioned her and my ankle paid the price, leaving me in a cast, and held hostage to my Dad's TV show choices. Ugh.

I knew I was in for long rounds of old Western reruns, and a lot of *NCIS*. Then he surprised me. He switched on a show called *Buy Alaska*. We watched five episodes, back-to-back. I was totally caught up in the romance (ha!) of off-grid living and the idea that there was a way to own land and still be free.

I announced to the living room that I was moving to Alaska.

I was convinced of this for a solid half-hour. Then I remembered that these shows are filmed in the spring and summer, and that living off-grid in the winter, in the freezing-ass snow and cold and having to fend off bears on the way to the outhouse was going to suck.

Which is when Hawaii said, hey, what about me?

And from that moment on, the doors flew off the hinges to get me here. I found a super cheap ticket, a large cash settlement I'd been waiting for from unemployment finally arrived, and one of my BFFs asked if she could take care of Lily the Incredible Traveling Cat[2] until her quarantine time was up. Within days, I found a position in marketing at Kalani, a Big Island retreat center in the Puna District. As my dream of 30 years was to open my own retreat center, this seemed ideal.

Turns out Kalani wasn't a good fit, but I found a house-sitting gig for the summer, by Ahalanui Warm Ponds. Being at Kalani gave me a chance to observe and start my list of what I will and won't do at my retreat center. Like if I'm promoting spiritual growth then a spiritual practice of some sort needs to be in place, not the antics of Club Med. No Mad Max at the Thunderdome gatherings in the back forty.

The island of Hawaii is considered to be an island of immediate manifestation, and in many ways, I'm watching that happen. After 23 months of court dates from hell back in California, I've received a substantial award check from my former employer.

Initially, I was tempted to spend the money on a couple of lingering bucket list items. I could buy a sailboat and cruise the South Pacific, or, buy my teardrop trailer to tow behind the Miata.

Just in time, I remembered the thing I came here for.

In this place, I get to live my wilderness girl, off-grid dream, like I was imagining I would do had I moved to Alaska.

So I, Wander Woman, am buying land.

What's cool is, friends and family will always have a place to come to, and I will always have a place to call home.

This is freedom. The randomness of my life that seemed chaotic and insane to those watching has a purpose, and this is it. I'm so glad I didn't settle for less.

Today I saw the dawn out my door and the ocean at my feet.
You may say I'm a dreamer…

---

[2] https://www.facebook.com/LilyTheIncredibleTravelingCat/

CHAPTER 2:
I Love Puna

Puna District is Not for the Faint of Heart

Living in Puna is not like living in the other districts on the island of Hawaii. Most districts have running water, electricity and cable, and county sewage or septic. Not Puna. There are no county trucks that come pick up our rubbish curbside, and in most cases, no mail delivery to our doors. There's not much recourse against the tweakers (meth/ice heads) and the rippers (thieves) who run rampant in certain areas, nonchalantly walking onto your property and leaving with whatever they can carry.

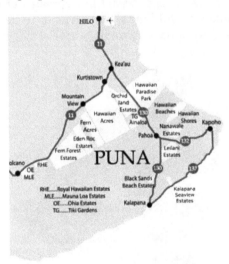

Map of the eruption area with street names and highways.

Puna, which is one of nine districts on the Big Island, is sometimes called the Wild West of Hawaii. This is because it's where people from other islands have been known to run to when they needed to hide. It's also where the ratio of police officers to population, and the amount of ground to cover, doesn't correlate.

It's also home to Uncle Robert's, an open-air market on sovereign land, that offers free live music on Wednesday nights.[3] It's the highlight of Puna social life. Because the land has been declared sovereign, they have their own system for registering vehicles, and identification (something that would later become a problem for those wanting to leave during the eruptions). It's also the location for Uncle's Awa (Hawaiian kava social and ceremonial drink) and Pakalolo (marijuana) bar with no harassment from outside law enforcement.

Puna is infamous for its vegan, tie-dyed, dreadlocked, barely clothed hippies (not all of them are this, some are garden-variety hippies, which is what my friends have called me). Otherwise known as Punatics. This is a good thing, or not, depending on who's saying it. That's the thing about Puna, it's contrary. There's a love for Kehena Beach, and for its clothing-optional drum circle on Sundays, but there's also a resentment regarding the nudity from families wanting to bring their keiki (children) for a Sunday picnic. It wouldn't be a big deal if we had more beaches, but we don't. Our coast is a rugged one, ever-changing from the ongoing lava flows from Kilauea, the battering it takes from deep-ocean currents, and an annual hurricane season that passes along our eastern-facing coastline.

Puna's population is around 50,000 but spread out over more than 300,000 acres. A friend once told me she has friends in Puna who've never been across the island to Kona, a two-hour drive. They live on their land, and that's where they stay.

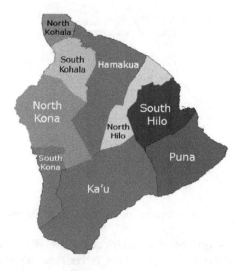

Boundaries of the 9 Districts on the island of Hawaii.

---

[3] https://sites.google.com/site/unclesawaclub/about-robert-keli-iho-omalu-sr

Besides having nine districts, Puna also has nine lava zones, and they don't line up accordingly because their boundaries shift with the eruptions. Most of Puna contains Lava Zones One through Three. My home in Lanipuna Gardens is in Lava Zone One.

Boundaries of the nine lava zones on the island of Hawaii.

It's hard to take this as a serious threat when what meets the eye are pristine jungles, quiet streets, established neighborhoods, and music festivals. It seems too magical to believe anything bad could happen here. Even though it has.

Puna and Lava

Kilauea has been erupting since 1983. In 1986, lava severed connection between Chain of Craters Road and Highway 130, and covered the community of Kapa'ahu, the village of Kalapana, and the subdivisions of Kalapana Gardens and Royal Gardens. During that time, the world-famous black sand beaches of Kaimu and Queen's Bath were taken.

More recently, in 2014, Kilauea threatened to cut off the highway between Hilo and Pahoa but stopped just short of the village (you can still see the hardened lava that was starting to ooze through the chain link fence at the Pahoa Transfer Station).

There were other volcanic events in the more distant past. The last time there were significant flows in the Lower East Rift Zone (LERZ) where my place is, was in the 1960s, and the lava covered Kapoho Village.

There was no flow when I bought my land, the lava being safely contained in the caldera of Kilauea. When it did flow, it was 20 miles away and cascading off a cliff into the ocean. If you don't live here this might sound scary, but it isn't. It's a uniquely beautiful natural occurrence and it seems like it could never come your way.

The gypsy wagon that would eventually become mine used to live in Kalapana.[4] That's where its creator, Aaron Anderson, built it and lived in it with his partner and two children. The wagon has also been home to The Hawaiian Hemp Council. There is actual documentary footage (I haven't seen it, a friend told me she saw it in her Hawaiian Studies class at University of Hawaii Hilo) of him pulling up stakes and driving the wagon out of the area as lava was approaching. It's passed through many hands since then, and back into Aaron's more than once, before its final landing with me.

Hawaiian legend says that if a home escapes the lava once, that it will be safe in future eruptions.

Other Things About Puna

We have one town, Pahoa Village. It boasts a hardware store, two auto-parts stores, a small library annexed to the school, a post office, a grocery, a health food store, Longs Drugs, and three banks. There are a dozen or so restaurants and the open-air market at Kalapana, and Maku'u. There is Ahalanui Warm Ponds and Pohoiki Beach Park. We also have the Awa bar and the Lava Museum. It's a village where, if you see someone in one of these places, you're bound to see them at the next. We all have the same errands to run, and in an area with sketchy Wi-Fi, the DVD rack at the library can be a busy spot.

All of this adds up to a type of freedom you don't find in most 'first world' locations. Whereas people on the mainland are having their property seized or condemned for living off-grid, we have no other choice. Where tiny homes are being banned elsewhere, we are finding loopholes. And while building with permits is advisable, in our land of long S-shaped driveways, what others can't see, won't hurt them. I can live in my gypsy wagon without being harassed. As can my friends who live in tents, treehouses, containers, yurts, and pallet constructs. Everything, ironically, but an RV, because Hawaii only allows in so many per year. Apparently, they're 'unsafe.'

We're living less-structured lives on purpose. I've been told I was living the dream. I agree, as long as that dream includes crawling out of my loft bed to go out in the pouring rain in the middle of the night to stand

---

[4] https://www.facebook.com/PunaGypsyWagon/

in the mud and pee.

How else could a Wander Woman commit to owning a piece of the planet?

Call me crazy, and I know some do, but my life, it rocks.

As I was driving down Pohoiki Road toward my street I started to get butterflies. Then when I turned onto my road, I broke into a huge happy face. Not that I wish I wasn't house-sitting in Kona, just that I remember how much I love this land. I love Pahoa. I get here and my heart sings. What is it about this place? I look around and wonder, is it our community? Is it the beauty of the wild rainforest? Is it the breath of Pele?

Yes.

8/21/15

When I was traveling in my first RV, in 2011, I loved the part about pulling into an RV park and beginning to set up. It was instant community. Strangers speaking to each other. What a concept.

This is what it's like in Puna. Tonight, I saw a woman parked at Longs, then again at Pahoa Fish and Chips. Instead of averting our eyes, we laughed. In the time it took for her to reach out her hand to shake mine, she'd told me her name, her profession, and what she'd done that day. And it's not creepy. It's not like she became my best friend and we stopped to braid each other's hair. She was gone minutes later. The longevity isn't the point. What mattered was the quality of the connection. This is Puna normal.

To be honest, I didn't really *love, love* Puna at first. I didn't get it. It took time to get used to the rugged coastline with its lack of typical, white, sandy beaches. Plus, mold. And the incessant singsong of the coqui frogs. And it's rural. Way rural. I've read articles about Puna back in the day when there were still sugar cane camps, and it's still got that feeling of being an older Hawaii than you get around the chain of islands.

Some people take offense to us saying we're Punatics, but no offense is meant. It's shorthand for, we know we're crazy for choosing to live this way, but we love it because it's magic. So, therefore, must we be.

We do have Wi-Fi in the jungle (sketchy when the wind blows). We have bylaws and building codes in subdivisions built on active volcanic rifts (some people even follow them). We have new and old hippies, we have Hawaiian locals, and wealthy imported retirees. There are a lot of hot guys who only have eyes for each other. We have shacks out on the lava and mansions on stilts next to the ponds. We have roads that end where the lava stopped less than a year ago. Because we live on the slopes of a live and active volcano; we live where Pele calls home.

I feel calm here. I like talking to strangers. I like forgetting what day it is. I like that after being here a short time, I run into people I know, or am about to know.

I'm an undomesticated human who drives her red convertible off-road in an untamed jungle.

It took some time for me to understand her nature, the nature of Puna and the jungle that is Puna. Now that I do, at least in a small way, I do *love, love* Puna.

4/24/18

I set monumental goals and I run with them. Then it hurts. Then I cry.
Then I regroup. Then I win. I'm like an opera.

Having things softer and easier for a few days while I was camping in Kona, at Magic Sands, offered me a much-needed rest, and a lovely little staycation. To be around people living mostly 'normal' lives, tourists out touristing, and to experience the ease that comes with warm and sandy beach strolls, all this helped to smooth some of my edges, which admittedly, have become a bit worn and ragged.

Because, for me, it is true that the grass looks greener on the other side. Which, ironically, is the side where I live. The east side, or Hilo side.

The green side. The rainy, muddy, lava-rocky side. The side where rain falls in buckets and lava flows in rivers. The side where the earth often rumbles and everything molds. Even the mold molds. The side where people dress in NOT their nicest clothes, and sometimes, their finest clothes have holes. Or they're wearing no clothing at all.

I live on the side where close to anything goes. The side where no one looks at you sideways when your land looks a mess, or when you're sleeping in your van while you're clearing and building and loving it. Or when you live in a tent, or in a tree, or like some, you hold your license plate on with a zip tie.

I live on the edgy side, with the other fringe dwellers. Punatics, all of us, marching to the beat of a drummer that only we hear. Nobody cares if you're tone deaf or can't carry a tune; because it's your personal song, and because they're marching too.

And of course, this is entirely true and utterly false. There are certainly people in Kona jiving to the music that only they can hear. And I know for a fact that there are people in Puna living perfectly 'normal' lives that are nowhere near the edge.

But there is also the song of a place, and we are drawn by those notes, because Its melody harmonizes with our own.

Puna is my melody. Kona is where I can rest, now and then, before jumping back into my own Puna jam. Or jelly, as it may be. LOL.

CHAPTER 3:
Retreat Center

8/25/15

I know that what I dream of is unrealistic. I know that some people might even resent what I'm trying to do, as if I'm taking shortcuts and not putting in the hard work it takes to own a piece of this planet. Yet, I don't want to own the planet.

I want to take all the things I've learned in order to survive my life and pay it forward.

I've been doing this all along, for decades. In crisis centers, at social services with juveniles on probation and their families, and with private clients. I've trained the people who work with them as well, so they can continue the services that we began. My dream has been to be able to do this in a bigger way, and to show you how you're on your own Hero's Journey. This is an Archetype, a universal pattern identified by Joseph Campbell in *Hero with a Thousand Faces*. According to his research documented by anthropologists and archeologists, in many different spiritual beliefs, we're all on a Journey, whether we know what that means or not.

I want to retrieve the Dark Night of the Soul from the arms of depression and realign it as your greatest gift. Understanding that the Dark Night feels different than depression and needs to be addressed from the perspective of a journey to be navigated, rather than an emotion to be endured. This empowers us to traverse the darkness that isn't a minefield so much as it is a gold mine of our true selves.

What I've envisioned is this retreat center, this place to come to for whatever amount of time you need, to live, to work, to rest, to rejuvenate, and to learn. It's not just my dream. What I've got mapped out on spreadsheets and in dozens of notebooks is a spiritual download. I say that because the breadth and scope of it is far too big for one person to have come up with on her own. I also say it because more times than I can count, I've encountered others with a similar vision, just none quite so thoroughly documented. This is a manifestation of what the planet is asking of us before we destroy ourselves and take her down with us.

Puna has the newest land on Earth, created by decades of constant lava flow. The air is the cleanest, the land the most alive. This is an opportunity to create space for a lot of people, who, with integrity and transparency, and our most earnest desires, can hold the highest intentions to evolve.

10/21/15

Live feed
https://www.youtube.com/watch?v=jDKOwdP2hrU&feature=youtu.be

…I got Title on my land today. My forever home. I'm giddy. I've lived a most precarious life until now. I've never felt the security of knowing my home can't be taken from me…

3/16/16

When it was time to invite people to move onto my land, I was completely transparent. If I'd read this, I'd have jumped on it, as many did, but very few wanted to do the actual work; instead, they wanted the fantasy. The reality of the mud and rain and hard work didn't fit in with their romantic notions any more than they did with my own.

The difference was, I owned this land, so I had a reason to see the investment through. I had a reason to look past the challenges toward my castle in the sky, which I knew I'd someday make come true. I believed in myself in the face of such challenges. For those who answered my ad, what they were looking for was an already built castle, which I couldn't provide.

This isn't an uncommon arrangement in Pahoa, where there are many work trades on farms and retreats. Nor is it a foreign idea for Wwoofers, those who find this a great way to travel and experience the world on a shoestring.[5] Pahoa attracts a lot of travelers and wwoofers, but I came to realize that after a while, many of them, young and able-bodied, found a way to qualify for social services, both money and foodstamps, and to not work at all. Of the ones who did want to work, they could pick and choose, and so they chose to go with indoor plumbing. Or any plumbing.

I had no idea what I was taking on, or how uphill I was going. Shrug.

The original ad from Craigslist:

- Hawaii >
- big island >
- wanted: roommates

This posting is from craigslist. [?]

---

[5] https://wwoof.net/#wwoof-start

[Posted 5 years ago]

Unique Communal Worktrade (Pahoa)
Unique communal work trade –

Just off Pohoiki Road I have an acre land parcel which I'm living on and developing into a spiritual retreat center. What I'm offering is a work exchange, 20 hours a week, in exchange for your labor of love in the tropical jungle of this beautiful island. I'm five minutes from Pahoa and just up the road from the Warm Ponds. This is an acre of lush and sacred space that is also an Adventureland of caves, lava tubes, craters, and deep rifts, and where, on a lucky day, you can catch fleeting glimpses of the Menehune at play.

Why you:

You are lighthearted, spiritually minded, and are a fellow explorer. You are kind. You have a great work ethic and you want to be part of a Big Vision. You are handy, you garden, build simple structures, or think that clearing land by hand (machetes and o'o bars) sounds like fun. Or maybe you have some unique talent that the world at large has mostly overlooked. When you were a kid you probably loved to build forts. And you have been a wanderer, wondering where your tribe is, or have only ever dreamed of what your ideal community would look like. What they would do, who you would be? If any of this describes you, you may have found what you've been looking for.

Why we fit:

The only thing constant in life is change. We all know that. We also know that we, and our planet, are in a time of great change. Affecting change requires consciousness, and intention. Affecting change as a group requires a shared vision, and a shit-ton of courage. You've also got to be a little bit insane, in a head on the ground, feet in the clouds, leap before you look kind of a way.

You've got to be willing to do things that your parents, co-workers, or whoever wrote the rules that you currently live by, probably don't want you to do. Not because you want to. Because you must.

Being part of a Big Vision means becoming part of the natural flow, and it means you keep moving, keep creating, and continue to turn over rocks in your search for more treasures.

Who I am:

I'm a lifelong learner with a slew of alphabet letters after my name, who, until now, was content with the life of a gypsy Wander Woman, solo traveling via trucks, trains, planes, and RVs. Through vision quests, monasteries, sailboats, shamanic descents, and playing with Fire, I've woven together my own Hero's Journey, in order to train and lead you and others, successfully, upon their own Heroic Path. I'm an Ecopsychologist who works with The Elements to hear, and to teach the language of things Other than Human, that until now has been part of our Wisdom disin-Heritage.

Healing. Creating. Evolving:

Coming to Hale Ōhana Honua is more than just finding a place to live. In return for your labor in service to the land, you'll have a tent to use if you need it, or you can build a small structure (treehouse?) to live in while you're here. Ever wanted to live in a cave? We've got those too.

We are building a mindful and intentional community of curious individuals, people who know that the sacred can be seriously funny, and that mindfulness includes stillness, as well as silliness, tiaras, and dress-up clothes. So, whether you're moving here fresh from the mainland and are looking for a place to land, or you've been here awhile but haven't yet found your tribe, this is a safe and sacred place to come to while you get your feet beneath you, and who knows, you may want to stay for more than a while.

For as long as you are with us, in return for your 20 hours per week you will receive:

- The use of a tent if you don't have one.
- At least one communal meal a day.
- Morning group meditation (don't worry, if you don't know how we'll teach you).
- Esoteric group discussion (and your chance to lead on a topic of your choice).
- The opportunity to become a long-term community member (ohana), once your probationary period is complete.
- Your Personal Element's Identification Profile.
- Hero's Journey Oracle Reading.
- Ongoing instruction about the Elements in your life and how to hear the voices of those other than human.
- Participation in all upcoming events.

We're at the very beginning of this project, so it's a bare bones operation. For this to be a good fit for you you've got to have the soul of an adventurer. A bit of Huckleberry Finn, Robinson Crusoe, and Peter Pan will do. Wouldn't hurt to have a dash of Zena and Buffy, as well.

A lot has happened in the 4 months since my escrow closed, but I won't kid you, we've got many miles to go. The great part is we'll be doing it together.

If this sounds appealing, and you're ready for the adventure of your lifetime, please send me an email with your resume and a letter, as brief or as lengthy as you'd like, telling me why this is for you. There is no wrong or right letter, and I won't be checking for grammar and spelling, I'll be listening for your heart and soul.

Thank you

- do NOT contact me with unsolicited services or offers

post id: 6318686204 posted: 2 years ago   updated: 2 years ago
email to friend 💜 best of [?]

[logged in as b***@gmail.com]   [log out]

CHAPTER 4:
Jungle Living

3/19/16

Phenomenal Power. Itty Bitty Living Space.

A dream is something you plan for, otherwise it's a fantasy.

Harsh judgment? Not really. Sometimes an awakening, a moment of epiphany, can sound like a judgment.

It's the middle of the night and I'm lying here listening to the sound of enormous drops of rain hitting the roof of my tent. Questioning every decision that got me here.

I've got cold feet. Literally. I got up to pee in my 'jungle bucket' and

stepped into a puddle of rainwater on my tent floor. Luckily, I did the wash today and easily found a fresh pair of dry socks in my laundry bag. We won't talk about how at least half of what's in there is also soaking wet.

What I want to do is cry, or swear, or scream, or run away. But it's raining and where would I go? I own this insanity. I bought it. On purpose.

Thank god my bed isn't wet.

Mostly not wet.

One pillow is soaked because it was on the edge of my sleeping pad.

Puna "jungle bucket" upgrade.

Having dry feet makes a world of difference. More than I'd have guessed.

It's still raining though so more than my feet could be cold and wet by the time the sun comes up.

This was never part of my glamping, spiritual retreat, tropical island fantasy. In that vision, I was always at the finish line. In all the years of creating this, I never considered the getting from point A to point B part. I didn't consider things like building platforms or punching through lava rock, or roaming black pigs squealing in the night, or fire ants, or the invasion of rats. Or of seeing coqui frogs over my head, crawling between the screen of the tent and the tarp. Or rain. Fucking rain.

I only ever saw the finished product and how happy we all were. All of us. Lots of us.

I wish I had more blankets. Blankets with dry edges. I wish I had a big, strong boyfriend who'd put his arms around me and tell me, "Go back to sleep, it'll be okay, Punkin', we've got this. I love you."

Apparently, I run more than one fantasy at a time.

Anyway, here I am. I'm living the invisible part behind stories of success and failure. The part where it looks and feels like a messy reality show kind of mistake. The part where the undisciplined and unmanageable fantastical dreamers consider throwing in the towel right before we're about to win. Right before the miracles happen.

Am I about to win? Hell, if I know.

I'm a creator. I don't hope for miracles; I rely on them. Because they happen. It's not true that this is all a fantasy. I've planned. I've collaborated with others. I've got the education and background and wealth of experience that supports my being able to run an amazing retreat center; and to do it successfully. I'm not as sure about the homesteading part. But it sounds like fun and like a challenge that can occupy my wanderlust for years to come.

The program is ready. This rainforest, lava, off-grid landscape is its perfect setting.

My vision is a massive one.

I'm a catalyst. I'm a trigger puller. I see the target and BAM! I take the leap from fantasy to reality.

Turns out, it's a wider gap than I expected. That leap I took feels like Alice must have felt as she went down the rabbit hole, head-over-heels, in a free fall with an assumption of landing softly.

I know nothing about clearing rainforest. Or leveling. Or building. Or lava. Or solar or catchment or cesspool or homesteading. I know a lot about camping but not a lot about what it feels like to wake up in the middle of the night, alone, with wet feet.

And, so far, I'm not doing what I came here for.

I didn't sign up for half a dream come true. Hear me, power greater than myself, it's time to kick down. Bring me the rest of the team. Get this place built. I dare you. Dammit and thank you.

3/24/16

"You are the dreamer. The master of the dream. Others may step in, with your permission, and you will share the vision. You get to delegate until you are sure they can be trusted to bring the vision full circle with you. You get to choose."
~ said a friend to me ~

I appreciate the wisdom in these words because this is a lot of work. I get tired. I wonder why I'm doing it. Then I think of the alternative which is wishing I'd done it...

Sometimes I comfort myself with the knowledge that I don't have to do this, that I can quit anytime. Like I'd do that. Ha.

The reality is, this vision, which until recently was only a figment of my imagination, is becoming a reality.

Another parallel reality is that there are a lot of moving pieces and navigating the people, places, and things of it are part of a pretty steep hands-on learning curve.

Each day becomes the next building block of a meditative practice in surrender, leadership, flexibility, boundary-setting, and self-care.

There's a third reality as well, which is, I don't want to manage people. I want to be a part of a greater whole, that's why I'm doing this! But, as it was pointed out to me above, it's my vision, so, at least in the beginning, I'm going to have to be in charge.

Okay, fine.

Meh.

An FYI for the future, this is it guys. This is the leap of all leaps, and good enough to satisfy even my thirst for adventure. From here on out its hammocks, sunbathing, and writing books.

> *A friend asked me how it feels to be where I'm at now, and what have I missed the most. Simple. Ice water. Dry clothes. Indoor plumbing. Coqui-free pillows.*

4/11/16

Water

Originally, I was going to call this essay "Poop and Maggots" but it's really about water. Running water. Hot, running water. On-demand, hot, running water. Turn the faucet and out it comes. No more poop and no more maggots.

Unfortunately, I haven't gotten that far yet. Although I'm told there's a meter somewhere around here, so running water does exist on my street. I'm also told I need at least one permitted structure in order to have it turned on.

Wondering what this has to do with poop and maggots?

Two words: Frankie. Lily. My ohana. Okay. Four words.

About this side of the dark side of the moon, during a light drizzle (thank god for once it was only light), I heard Frankie whining. I leapt out of bed because I know what that means, I've got to poop, Mom. Not usually a problem but he ate late. By the time I get to him. Poop. Handfuls of it in the dark. Under my nails. On everything.

Sanitized wipes and what water was left in my five-gallon Igloo, plus some rain buckets, got me and Frankie cleaned up, and the poop pile far away and ready for the laundromat at dawn.

Back to bed. But wait.

Mush between the toes. Eww. Cat barf. Dammit Lily! Stop eating the freaking coqui frogs. Oh. Way more eww. The barf was already teeming with writhing, freaking maggots. By now I'm out of water, and there goes the last of the sanitized wipes.

The good news? I'm not the first, nor the last homesteader/off-gridder to have a night like last night. Frankie, my five-month-old pit bull, and Lily, my 12 year-old gray tabby, both seem okay today. My nails are clean. As is the rest of me. Thanks to my BFF Mitchel, whose career includes manager of floor design for Macy's, the wash is done, and he made me laugh. And I'm in Hawaii. And my friend Mac was here while I was out, working in the rain on my halfway-built platform. He also made me smile. I'll have a flat, dry, solid surface soon. Wow! The things we take for granted.

This shall all pass. Except the living in Hawaii thing. And the solid outpouring of aloha from friends and new acquaintances I've been blessed to receive.

And one day, I too shall have running water. Hot AND cold. On demand. Water.

One of us underestimated me...could have been me.

4/12/16

My Grandma Cherole (Gram) told me I was meant to climb mountains. She taught me to meditate when I was seven. She also told me about Atlantis, reincarnation, and Edgar Cayce. She cultivated my curiosity and taught me how to think outside the box long before I knew that boxes existed.

She taught me to trust myself. She pointed at the horizon and said it was mine.

There were other women too in my family who taught me wise things, like women are strong and smart and brave. Women can camp and sail boats and catch fish. That men and women are equal.

Grandma Cherole.

As I sit in my tent tonight, on the eve of my one-month anniversary of jungle living, I'm thinking of them all, but I'm especially thinking of my Grandma Cherole.

More than anything else, what I got from her is that I am meant to be fearless.

Sometimes I'm afraid, but that's different than being fearless. Fearless means I can trust myself. I trust that if I fall, I'll get back up. I trust that if I'm hurt, I will survive, as long as I get back up. I trust that everything I do now is a culmination of mastery from past lives and the continuance into the next.

I've taken any number of great leaps into the unknown, so many that it doesn't scare me the way that maybe it should. I sure as heck have dark moments when I think, WTF was I thinking? But then the moment passes, leaving behind the next important understanding I'd have otherwise missed. And I remember why I continue to leap.

I think the greatest gift I have to offer is to pass that gift of inspiration on to you.

I'll never push you off the cliff. I might point the way. You can choose to leap. Or not.

Sometimes, after a lifetime of mountains, the road less traveled is the one that looks too easy. Then, you realize, they're all mountains in the beginning.

4/15/16

I was on a plane that got hijacked. A sick child was on board. She was growing a skin cover over her body. As time passed it began to extend over others, so they were all encased together inside this undulating, sac-like layer of skin.

Beneath the layer they could no longer communicate. They were muffled. Stifled. All you saw was movement under this terrifying skin sac.

I had an idea for a solution but thought it was so obvious that someone must already know. Or else they'd already tried it and it didn't work. So, I kept my mouth shut.

Finally, I spoke up. Turns out no one had thought of my idea. They were excited.

The problem was solved.

This is what I do. What I've always done. I underestimate what I see. I believe everyone knows more than me. I see simple solutions to complex problems and dismiss them because of their simplicity. I give the beliefs of the majority permission to stifle my individual voice.

This dream is a metaphor for an authentic life, painted in the broadest of strokes. It reminds me of something Mahatma Gandhi said, "Just because you're a minority of one the truth is still the truth." Or, as it is often misquoted, just because you're a minority of one does not mean you are wrong.

The Message: Say it anyway.

The Mission: Allow the solution to be simple. The hijackers are powerless.

The Moral: We're taught that life is hard. What if we were misinformed?

CHAPTER 5:
Gypsy Wagon

3/31/17

I love this old gypsy caravan.

I love that there's no hum of electricity. I love the quiet beneath the cacophony of 10 thousand boy coqui frogs begging the 10 thousand silent girl coquis to please let them get lucky tonight. I love the muddy, clean scent of the air from my jungle, and from the ocean as it washes up the valley from the Puna coastline. I love how my body can feel at rest, away from all things electronic.

Meeting the Wagon

When my neighbor first told me he had a trailer I could borrow for a few months, I thought, that's really nice, and this is Puna, and it's probably a rust bucket. Why would a stranger offer me a perfectly good place to live, for free, if it was a perfectly good place to live?

So, I said thanks, and I'd walk over and check it out when I had time.

A week later, my neighbor came by again to say he really thought I should go check it out. This time I couldn't squirm out of it, and I had two new people with me who'd answered my ad to work trade, so we went. His driveway is gated, and beyond that is a small incline, which he said to follow. That I couldn't miss the trailer.

It was hot, and I was irritated, and it was nagging at me that nothing is ever free. Thoughts I was sharing with my two new friends as we approached the top of the incline. Then I saw it. Not a trailer. A gypsy wagon. A domed, tiny home with a hitch. Only something I'd created an entire Pinterest album for a few months back.

I forgot about my concerns in my excitement about the wagon, and at seeing yet another one of the pieces of my life landing so neatly into place.

I had my land. I had workers. I had a gypsy wagon. I had plans.

Moving the Wagon Home

No way was I going to be able to pull the wagon with the Miata, so I hired someone. My driveway in was mostly clear of stumps, and I knew exactly where I wanted it. All of which I explained to the guy I hired. But who am I to suggest we take out the remaining stumps before we try backing it in? Just because I had the tools in my hands was no reason to stop now.

So, in he backed, and boom. Stuck. And he wants to know what we should do now. Umm. I already made my suggestions. What do YOU think YOU should do now? And wasn't his truck four-wheel drive, couldn't he put it in gear and pull it back out? Nope.

Who on earth moves something this size, this heavy, over muddy ground, with two-wheel drive? He decides he'll come back tomorrow with a borrowed truck and a house jack.

And before I could suggest putting blocks beneath the back of the wagon, which only sat on one axle, it's unhitched, butt up in the air.

The following day I asked Mac, my friend who's building my platform, to supervise while I stayed far away. He called me when they were done, to tell me it was all good now, and that yes, it was balanced and stable. But still next to the crater, which was not where I wanted it.

I want to be out in the sunshine. I want to open my door and see my glorious jungle. I do not want to be hovering over a 50-foot crater, under 100-foot trees! And hell, if it's balanced.

It wobbles. And when it wobbles, I can see straight into the crater, and the puka, the lava tube in the center.

But Mitchel said he'd help me, so we went to the Transfer Station for treasures. I told the guys who work there, who had already helped me so much with tents and tarps, about my wobbly wagon. One of them, Martin, offered to bring his house jack in the morning and help me get safe.

When he arrived in the morning, he said, oh, this is THE wagon! And he

Frankie in front of the wagon before it was leveled.

told me the story of meeting Aaron Anderson, the wagon's builder, decades ago while hitchhiking on the mainland, then again, a couple of years later when he flew into Hilo. And that this is the wagon Aaron built.

That's how I began to gather stories of the wagon. Or tried. Many people were excited to say they'd been in it, even lived in it, but very few were willing to part with the details. My own den of iniquity.

It became enough for me to admire it for its notoriety, and its history, and once Mitchel and Martin got it up on blocks, I no longer had to be afraid of wobbling or rolling into the crater.

My friend Dee came to help me clean, to put tarps over the missing skylight to dry it out inside, and to set up the outdoor kitchen which was under the awning created by my loft bed.

With Mitchel's decorating expertise, we made it beautiful, with satin curtains, a blue ottoman, and a pile of blankets and futons. My friends Linda and Steve added in a beautiful felted rug, my neighbor made me a bamboo lamp filled with fairy lights, and Mitchel hung a privacy tarp across the front entrance of my "driveway," which was now blocked by the wagon.

Mitchel lounging in the loft after he finished decorating my hale.

And then the real adventures began.

Coquis Love the Wagon

Coqui frogs used to only live on the island of Puerto Rico. Then Walmart failed a few container inspections and the coquis came to Hawaii. Now the once silent nights are full of the coqui mating call, and it's estimated there are about 20,000 per acre.

One of countless coquis on my 'catch and release' plan.

There weren't quite that many inside my wagon, it only sounded like it. I didn't mind finding gecko eggs, I relocated those, but I still knew too little about the coquis to realize I should be looking not just for renegade frogs, but for their egg sacs as well. I was about to learn.

In Puerto Rico, the coquis are quite small, and their population is manageable. In Hawaii, where they have no natural predators besides chickens, they've grown to at least twice the normal size. And they are loud. Bloody freaking loud, and inside the wagon, they echo.

They would wait until I turned off my hurricane lamp before starting their call. Or before jumping next to my head onto my pillow. I could usually tell when one was nearby by watching where Lily was looking.

I tried to find them before turning out the lights. I pulled out drawers and moved my small clothes dressers to find them. I used a glass jar to catch them, and I got a pasta grabber, you know those claw looking things, to pick them up so I could throw them out the door into the jungle. Every time I thought I had them all, and I could sleep, I shut off the light...and...coqui, coqui!!![6]

What was loud outside was a deafening echo inside.

Then one night it began to rain, and I felt a water drop on my arm. I rolled my eyes, thinking I had another leak to repair as I turned on the light to deal with it.

It wasn't rain. I really should have looked for those egg sacs. You see, coquis are born fully formed, and the size of a pencil eraser. By the light of my lamp, they were boinging everywhere. I don't know how many. A lot. It was too hot to sleep with the sheet over my head, and I was afraid without it they'd jump in my mouth and up my nose.

So, I caught them. One by one. I flung them into the jungle. I told them to warn their cousins of the dangers in the wagon.

---

[6] https://www.youtube.com/watch?v=54-FzuE-w0U

It didn't end there. I'm a coqui magnet. They jump on my legs when I'm sitting outside. They find me. They sit outside my door and wait for me to come home. They taunt me. They lay their eggs in my kitchen. Not one of them has turned out to be a prince. To be clear, I haven't tried kissing any of them so I may have blown my chance.

A tiny, elderly, Asian woman at the Transfer Station once told me the way she gets rid of them is with boiling water.

I'm going to stick with my pasta claw for now.

How the Wagon Became My Permanent Home

When Raj, my neighbor, first offered me the wagon, he was lending it. But after he saw the work we put into it, and how much I loved it, he said it was mine.

I found out years later that it wasn't his to give, that it belonged to a woman who had lived on his property and left, abandoning it, so I guess it was okay. That's kind of the life this wagon has led. Passed from one to another, sometimes borrowed and sometimes sold. Until she landed with me.

I wish my wagon could have told me the stories that the people I met were so reluctant to share.

CHAPTER 6:
Recommitting

7/5/16

Living with the Menehune

Last night there was a whole lot of rattling in my kitchen. As my kitchen is outside, and right below my loft window, the rattling was LOUD. It sounded like rats. Big squeaky ones. With sharp nails scraping across my glass jars of turmeric, and of honey. I yelled at them to leave. I blew my air horn. I heard them scatter across the tables and tarps. You'd think that Frankie might have barked but he didn't stir, and Lily, the mad rodent catcher of yesteryear, sat placidly, watching out the window.

My wagon kitchen is almost set up. My loft bed above in the overhang. What a view of the jungle I had.

Finally, I fell asleep, only to suddenly wake up a little before midnight, wondering what had disturbed me.

Then I heard footsteps run across my front steps and thought, was that black pigs? We had discovered a large nest of them in the back of my jungle, and I often heard their echoing squeals, but rarely did they come up front. And then my door flew open.

Pigs don't open doors, especially my door, which is secured from the inside with a bungee cord. My door flew open like it was on a spring. WTF. I didn't feel scared, I felt confused. I lit my hurricane lamp as I climbed down from the loft to shut it again. I double-checked to make sure it was properly secured before climbing back into bed.

Frankie, my eight-month-old pit bull, still wasn't barking, which is unusual because he likes putting on his big-boy bark when the pigs come around. Lily, who never meows, or gets excited for that matter, was being very alert and watching from the edge of the bed. Did they know something I didn't?

The door flew open again. Four times. Not with footsteps, just a BOING, and the door flying open.

Now my heart was racing. WTF was going on? Was it kids having a prank on a full moon night in the jungle? Couldn't be because they'd have made more noise. Sound carries a long way in the jungle and from my perch in the loft I can hear everything, and there were no giggles, or "oh craps" from tripping over stumps. There was nothing. I've also got tin roofing laid all around to combat the mud and stop the jungle growing on the pathways, so it's impossible, especially in the dark, to walk anywhere at my place without a cacophony of metal clangs.

Before you ask, yes, the bungee cords were solid, as were the knobs I had them hooked to. What was going on?

I asked.

Out loud.

"What's going on? What do you want from me?" And because I asked, I was answered.

It was the mischievous energies I'd felt when I first met my land. It was the Menehune, the Trickster, my amakua, from the age of three, when Coyote came to me in a dream, that wasn't a dream. I may have been three, but I know a live animal when I see one. Here they were again, trying to get my attention to address an imbalance.

Being in alignment with the aina, means being in alignment with its spirit inhabitants.

I'd encountered the Menehune last summer, when I began looking for my land.

I was house-sitting in Leilani Estates. I'd fall asleep at night and there they would be, squatting on my chest with their hands around my neck. I knew this wasn't a malevolent gesture, and even though it was scary, I understood they were trying to get my attention.

Apparently, they felt I couldn't listen properly without an element of terror involved.

After a few nights of this, I was pissed. I'd also started catching glimpses of movement out of the corner of my eye at dusk, a time they are known for appearing. When it happened again, I told them to get the fuck off me. Literally, in those very words. That if they have something to say to me to find another way. They were shocked—I could feel their astonishment, but they got off of me.

Right about now I imagine you're thinking, uh huh, she's crazy...

But think about this. We've all had experiences where something we can't explain in 'rational' terms has happened. We may dismiss it but that doesn't mean it didn't happen. It just means we can't explain it. Eventually we get the message, or the spirits, or whatever they are, give up on us as a lost cause and move on to someone who will listen.

When I found what was to become my place, I could feel their energy at play. It wasn't mean-spirited, but it felt like they'd been alone for a very long time and had gotten bored. The energy felt mischievous and my first inclination was to say, "Hell no!" Then go look someplace else. Which I did.

When I changed my mind and decided that it was, in fact, the Place for me, I asked for their protection and cooperation in exchange for my stewarding the land.

As long as I've been living alone here, I've had only the cooperation and protection of them. Until last night.

In the last few weeks, people came here who didn't belong. They didn't stay. They were fearful, angry, and judgmental. They saw things, things that scared them, and drove them away within days. They left, but they disrupted our jungle flow. It got on the place, and it got onto me. And I was being called to account for it.

I acknowledged this. I answered for my part in inviting them here. I knew it was up to me to make things right and would my words be enough? To say it is my kuleana to malama the aina, and to ask if we were pono? I accepted this responsibility to care for the land, and could I make it right again?

Would this restore the imbalance? Would the spirits of my land feel my commitment?

Guess so, because after that, my door stayed shut and I went to sleep.

Most everyone who came to my land, either to work or to stay, had unexplainable experiences. My island friends of Hawaiian descent could feel the elders in the ohia trees and in the land.

Whatever anyone saw reflected who they were in the world. I know that one woman saw thieves going through our things, but I could see the entire camp from my loft, and no one was there. She left the next day, angry with me.

Both of my hired workers had experiences as well. One heard a voice coming from the back and he said it sounded like they were stealing. But there was no way to get back there until we created a way. And stealing what? Jungle vines and cane grass? The other saw his Tutu, chanting and nodding her approval. He said she'd passed away 10 years before and this was the first time he'd seen her since. That she approved of my being here and of what he was doing.

Call this what you will, just don't miss the message along the way. Our alignment is connected to everything around us. If something is out of whack, so will the rest be. As everything is conscious, according to its function and form, it's to our benefit to learn to pay attention to and address the imbalance. To be pono.

Even if it looks like we're only talking to thin air.

Your greater purpose is none of your business.
Just do the next right thing. Even if it doesn't make sense.
Especially if it doesn't make sense.

7/11/16

The Art of Aloneness

I'm very good at being alone.

While reading today at the pond someone came up to tell me that I read too much and it's because I'm afraid of having my own adventures in real life. I laughed out loud.

As if.

But it made me stop to consider something else. As a child I was isolated. I was on the fringes of my family, the perpetual watcher. I immersed myself in the life of whatever book I was reading in order to get away from the violence and the loneliness of how it felt to live inside that house.

My person. Me. Who felt unloved and unlovable. The me who saw things differently than the people around me. The me who got strange looks for saying what I saw. The me my family said was born at the wrong time because they couldn't understand me. They wanted my ideas to go away. To not question the status quo. To keep life simple. On their terms.

I transcended that isolation in my late teens through work and my boyfriend and his Porsche. I cut school. I adventured. I came out of my cocoon and a few years later, emerged into my social butterfly-ness as a cocktail waitress and bartender.

Except it all revolved around partying. And I didn't understand some parts of that life. I mean, if we were late for the concert already, why did we have to chase down drugs first? It was the eighties, I lived in Marin County, where cocaine flowed like water from the tap, but did we have to miss the show to go get more? Couldn't we do it later?

Apparently, I didn't understand addiction.

I retreated into aloneness. I traveled. I moved. I adventured. But I didn't deeply connect with anyone. Aloneness was a lot like my isolation, but I called it independence, and I didn't know how to change it. I tried to learn how by reading more books. Instead of fantasy science fiction I hit the "shelf"-help section. I'm pretty sure I read them all. I wanted to understand.

I think that some of my loneliness was about choosing the road less traveled. If I once learned how to not be alone, I've forgotten it along the way. I am invited places, or not, and sometimes I go, but more often, I don't. The paradox is that when I'm not invited, I feel left out. I want to be invited but rarely do I want to go.

Today my son told me that I AM the red-headed stepchild. That I will always say things that will be misunderstood. That I will always see things before most people see them. Plus, says my wise son, you're also the black sheep. Just accept it. And breathe.

While I do enjoy my own company and I love to immerse myself in books, I'd also like to be less alone.

So, if you see me sitting in my car at the pond, book in hand, it's cool to say "hi." I'm not being afraid of living beyond what my book can offer, nor do I think I'm better than you. More likely I'm a socially awkward adventurer who's gotten too good at being alone.

7/20/16

Did things have to be this difficult? No. I don't think they had to be.

Then why have they been?

First, living in the jungle hasn't actually been that hard on me. The hardest part, really, has been enjoying the wild and crazy adventure of it, without your approval.

A little backstory to fill in the blanks...

I learned to read at a very young age. I was inspired by *Green Eggs and Ham*. I loved that book. I begged everyone to read it to me repeatedly. I begged so much they got tired of it and told me to read it to myself. When I was three years old, that's what I did, I taught myself to read starting with, "Do you like" and "Sam I am." "Would you" and "could you" were slightly more challenging.

By the time I was six, I was given access to most of the school library. I loved autobiographies and anything adventure. My favorites included *The Boxcar Children*, *The Land of Oz*, and of course, *The Hobbit* and *Lord of the Rings*. I also read other classics, like *Robinson Crusoe*, and *Swiss Family Robinson*.

Do you get where I'm going with this?

The books I read were always about surviving hardship, going on a Hero's Journey, and emerging triumphant. They were about making do with what was at hand. Making something from nothing. They were about mysterious places, creatures, and people who weren't like me. They were about pitting yourself against unforeseen challenges and failing, until you emerged victorious. They were about finding out what you are made of.

So maybe...no, definitely, I created that for myself here in the jungle. I'm not actually stranded on a desert island. There aren't any cannibals on their way to eat me and most of the foraging I do is at the farmer's market.

But.

I get to experience those childhood dreams and to find out if I can, in this day of modern conveniences, survive without the things that make life easier.

What I've discovered is, I am stronger than my fear of being alone in the dark, and of enormous roaming black pigs that go bump in the night. I can kill my own flying cockroaches with the bump on the side of my closed fist. I can also talk myself off the ledge when trees fall, rain pours, winds howl, doors fly open, and when all doesn't go according to plan. And, I can take cold showers in the sunshine.

Most of all I've found I can be content and at peace with very little. I can live without Netflix.

The biggest challenge I've faced is reconciling the way I've been living with the way of the world around me. It's confusing to be content one moment, then feel the lack of what's missing in the next.

I think I've blundered upon the crux of the situation: I can't be both hermit and social being at once. Finding the place where the two intersect could be a worthy, or a futile endeavor.

Even *Green Eggs and Ham* is about trying something new and finding out it's not bad.

My time of metamorphosing alone in the rainforest is coming to conclusion. My time of being goo inside the caterpillar cocoon is peaking.

Once upon a time I got curious about what happens inside of the cocoon, so I looked it up. What I learned is that when the caterpillar goes into its cocoon it isn't just to take a nap and grow a set of wings. Its metamorphosis is absolute. Inside that tiny casing the caterpillar is reduced to a soupy goo, a goo made of imaginal disks.

The imaginal disks hold the memory of what the caterpillar is to become.

Does it know when it goes in that it's going to come out a butterfly? Does the butterfly know it hasn't always been able to fly? Do they know of each other at all? Are they each other's memories, in the same way that we remember being a different person today than we were a year ago, or five?

They probably don't know any of this anymore than we do, when we get reduced to goo. I believe we also have imaginal disks, and when we feel like we've been reduced to goo, they are remembering forward on our behalf.

Metamorphosis isn't pretty. Goo is unavoidable. How much time we spend in the cocoon may be negotiable.

*The jungle has reclaimed its own. The platform is barely visible.
It's impossible to get to my shower. I thought I'd feel bad about this
but instead it feels good again. Like all the weird energy from the people
who didn't work out has been washed away. Time to begin again.*

CHAPTER 7:

Crazy

8/9/16

That dream you have, you know, the secret one you think is a little crazy. It's your gift. A thing is only crazy until somebody does it and it works. Then everyone's doing it, and it's only the crazy ones who aren't.

Two months ago, my dream of building a retreat center miraculously came to life. For three whole days. When it abruptly ended, I received advice from three of my aunts.

- Aunt E. suggested I rethink my goals.
  What I heard was, give up, you can't do this, be safe, be reasonable, be logical, you can't do this crazy thing you're doing.

- Aunt M. suggested I get off my land and house-sit.
  What I heard was give up, be safe, you can't do this, it's too hard, it's impossible and you're incapable of pulling off this impossibly huge idea, which was a fantasy anyway and for someone smarter and better than you.

- Aunt J. suggested I not give up because she's seen more miracles happen for me than for anyone she knows. She said she'd never have taken on something like this but it's exactly the kind of thing I'd do.
  What I heard was, you're crazy, it looks impossible from here and I'd never do it, but don't give up because you've done lots of crazy and impossible things, against all odds, and made them come true.

It all stung. Although it felt good to know someone besides me had noticed the miracles.

It's just...I don't want to always be the woman pulling a rabbit out of her hat. I sometimes want to be normal. Riiiiight.

The sting was in the words that echoed the ones floating around in my own head. I'm too old, too weak, too confused, too incapable, too hard to live with, and live in too much of a fantasy world. That what I imagined I could do was too unrealistic, and fantastical, and years too late.

I was also chastising myself for having spent my money unwisely, (why didn't I buy that sailboat or teardrop trailer to travel around the mainland, or just buy a round-trip ticket to the world?).

Who was I to think if I built it, they would come?

Playing the cards where they lay.

In the end, they did me a favor. While my Aunts may have tapped into things I thought but wasn't saying, the fears they were voicing were their own—I don't have to own them. I can choose.

Fear is a magnetic force that attracts more fear and repels abundance. Stubbornness, in the face of obstacles and challenges, obliterates wisdom and vision and blinds us to other options.

My options:

- Give up and sell my land. Cut my losses and run.
- Move off my land and house-sit where I've got Wi-Fi and electricity and can complete my oracle deck, make money, then pay to have all the things done to the land that I can't do myself.
- Cut and run. I know I already said that, but it comes up twice as often as everything else.
- Slow this whole process down. Live simply, don't pin my hopes on anyone staying. This is my dream.
- Cut and run.
- Believe.
- Write my book.

Everything you see around you today was once someone's crazy dream. We need the crazy dreamers. I'm not saying we live our lives for someone else as some sort of martyr. I'm saying that in living our lives out loud we never know who will hear us and because of what they hear, become part of the changes we want to see in the world.

The biggest gift we can give to ourselves is to live our lives authentically. To be who we secretly dream of being. There is no act of service more generous than to be who we are.

The world needs your gifts. We need your dreams. Yes. You.

Feeling like a fraud isn't normal. It's merely common.

8/23/16

I love you. And honestly, I'm in so much pain, I don't know how to keep on keepin' on.

It's the emotional beat down that's become intolerable. It may be that the relentless physical pain isn't helping.

I've managed to make it six months, living off-grid, alone, in the Puna rainforest on the Big Island of Hawaii. Against the odds, and the opinions of many people, I've made it. I've survived my 24/7, six-month-long vision quest. And I feel like it has perforated my soul.

I'm tired. Tired of being sick, tired of being alone, tired of the rain, tired of not having a flush toilet, tired of no electricity or Wi-Fi so I can work, and tired of being on a learning curve that even my stubbornness is flailing against. I'm tired of judgments, and resentments, and being the never-ending trigger, and catalyst, for other people's shit. I'm tired of men who say they care, who extend a helping hand, then slap me when I reach out to accept. And I'm tired of being blamed for how some people feel when they measure themselves against me, and feel they've come up short.

I'm just a quirky, curious human, driven by an eccentric soul, who thought that this would be a good lifetime in which to push some limits, and some boundaries, and to break a few rules. To cry when things got hard, then, almost as soon as things turn around, get back on my feet and do it all over again. And again. And again.

I'm afraid I've worn myself out. I'm afraid this vision of 30 years, of having my own healing retreat in the jungle, well, that it was just a dream. I'm afraid that all the planning, all the self-work I've done, and all the work I've done in support of others, has been a waste of time. And that my desire to pay forward what I've learned has been an ego trip.

I wanted to show you that if you set your mind to it that anything can be done.

I'm afraid I may be proving the opposite.

I wanted a community, but nobody stays. I wanted to help others heal by being on my land and offering them the wisdom of my experience and education.

I can't stand the alone.

I'm broke. Broken.

My health and stamina are like the rifts my land is littered with. The tears that are caught in my throat threaten to choke me.

My wise son says I'm one of those people who lives their life solely for the human experience. The entire spectrum of it.

Normally you'd hear something like this in the middle of an inspirational book, right as things turned themselves around for the heroine on her journey. You'd know there was a promise of a happier ending. I'm sorry I can't give that to you. Not yet anyhow.

8/24/16

I needed that level of exposure I shared with you yesterday. I needed my rawness to be at your mercy. If only so I would no longer be in it alone. Only my own words could shred me so completely. Only by my own hand could I say the things that would leave my psyche so undressed.

I've run my soul ragged by clinging to dreams and beliefs that weren't mine to hold but had been given to me, the ancestral baggage I was handed at birth. Or before. The silently beseeching words so carefully chosen to fool me into thinking I was one of you.

I'm not. One of you. Or even one. I'm all of you. We're all of us. The rest is smoke and mirrors diverting us from the pain of separation and our longing to come together. And our fear that if we do it will tear us apart. Like we'll disintegrate into nothingness without our things around to define us. To remind us of who we think we are.

But we aren't. We aren't bankers or hippies or failures or successes. We are souls having a human experience. It's only our human selves that think otherwise.

I've exposed myself, and yet I still cling to my treasured treasures, scattered around my rainforest. They nag at me. They say tend to me. They say look at us, don't look at you. Don't leave the human condition. It's not allowed.

And I don't want to anymore. I don't want to heal. I'm sick and fucking tired of 'healing.' I'm not broken. You're not broken. Our experiences, with whatever labels they are given, are all part of us, not good things to keep, or bad things to throw away. Our emotions aren't a tray of beads to be separated by color, but rather strung together on endless strands.

Strife and angst exist because we are in collusion with the illusion. It's all made up. The rules, the contracts, and the credit scores. All out of a misplaced concept of safety. As if we are in danger.

As if.

I don't know what's next. I'm shocked at the distance I've found between me and you. My insides hang, like musty layers of crumpled clothing, awkward and uncomfortable.

I'm incongruent with my history. I know this, I've felt it. I've tried to navigate it. The paradox of needing, and not needing. And the silence around me as I wait for what's next. Will I do it again? Has my epiphany or my discomfort altered my course?

It would be a supreme waste to turn away from the darkness, purely for the sake of the light. Our most precious and vulnerable parts have taken refuge in shadow, and only by looking directly into our pain can we hope to regain what we've lost.

Will life change swiftly or continue as it has, the only difference being that now I think I know why I suffer?

I'm on the upswing of this emotional roller coaster and focusing on creating new dendrites in my neural pathway.

CHAPTER 8:
Why I Stay

11/13/16

People ask me why I stay. Or why I did it. Or how I did it.

By putting one foot in front of the other. By adapting. By rolling with the punches. By not giving in to the jungle. By not giving up when people disappointed me. By laughing and crying and swimming and sleeping and writing, and by remembering my dream. By trying new things when old things didn't work. By accepting help when it is offered.

How did it happen this way?

It was never my intention to live alone in the jungle. I had an intermittent house-sitting job lined up that was supposed to carry me through the summer while I developed my land.

I had someone who knew the jungle who was supposed to move onto the land. My son was thinking of moving here. I had a friend who wanted to live here, but when she did finally land, was gone three days later. I had work trade people who didn't work. I had so many people come and go. Each time I got my hopes up. Each time I got the rug pulled from beneath me.

But.

Each time, in between the comings and goings, a bit of progress would happen. I counted on miracles, and as usual I wasn't disappointed. They kept me going through the leaky roofs, falling trees, and the chronic pain.

My savings were dwindling. And with limited electricity and Wi-Fi, I couldn't move forward on projects with the momentum that I had in the beginning. I couldn't tackle both the jungle and write a book. Because of my health I couldn't take a job.

I lived in the jungle in my gypsy wagon for six months this way. And then I couldn't do it anymore.

One day I found myself hyperventilating in the outdoor shower that I loved, because the weeds had grown two feet tall between it and my doorstep in two days. I was literally wailing into the jungle, my cries echoing back to me my despair. I had to catch myself.

I was afraid I'd pass out and no one would find me until years later because the weeds would have grown entirely over me within 24 hours.

I made my way back to my wagon and sat on the steps. Dazed. What was I going to do now?

I asked, (wailed) out loud. "What do you want me to do?"

What I got back was, "GET OFF THE LAND. GO HOUSE-SIT. RECUPERATE. GIVE YOURSELF A BREAK."

Yes. I have a booming voice that lives on my land. A few months ago, it had told me to "GO TO THE POND!" I argued then too, that I had too much to do, but the booming voice insisted, so I went. It turned out that many good things would happen at the pond, like lifelong friendships, and the heat of the geothermal water easing the pain in my body. And when I was betrayed by someone I loved, it was the place that I went to heal.

I decided I should listen to the booming voice again.

I got off the land. I posted an ad on Craigslist and someone in Kona found me the next day. They needed me right away. Frankie moved to Mitchel's, where he already had his extended pack of dogs. He's happy there. Two days later, Lily and I drove across Saddle Road on Mauna Kea, just ahead of an impending hurricane, through torrential rain, lightning strikes, and gale-force winds. Just another day in paradise.

That was two months ago.

For the first few weeks, I never left the house. Not exactly true. I went outside to feed the dogs and to bring them upstairs in the afternoon. I walked in the gardens. I coveted the not yet ripe avocados hanging within arm's reach. I drank ice water. I turned on lights by flipping switches. I walked down the hallway to the bathroom instead of driving down to the Beach Park or copping a squat with my jungle bucket. I rested. I cooked. I worried about setting up my computer and getting to work but didn't have it in me yet.

For those two weeks my car stayed in the driveway, the white sandy beaches not enough to lure me out of this rest I so sorely needed.

With time, I gained a new perspective on what I'd just done. That this six-month vision quest I'd been on, following the trajectory of an archetypal Hero's Journey, needed time to be assimilated. Which I've been doing. I've made a start of it at least, and I feel human again. Not so raggedy at the seams. I feel ready to begin again.

I also got some work done. A lot, actually. My oracle deck, Meeting the Mentor: Conversations with Pele, is ready for use, and approaching publication.

I'm going to California in December for a month to continue my recovery from Phase One of Corey of the Jungle. I have a house-sitting gig set up for February back here in Kona.

Phase Two is about cash flow and paying people to do what isn't in my wheelhouse. I write the programs. I facilitate them. I ask you the questions you don't want to answer but are afraid you'll never be asked. I don't homestead.

Many people have asked me why I don't give up. In their minds it's too hard. Impossible even. They want my life to be easier.

The reason I don't give up is because this isn't a one-night stand kind of dream.

I allowed myself to be distracted by the *Robinson Crusoe* adventure of it all, I lost sight of my true goals and I took things personally that weren't. My land is a place for deep-dive retreats. It makes sense that I'd have to go on one first in order to understand what my land has to offer.

Resistance to the situation is what causes the pain. It's time to go all zen and shit.

I need to have fun. I need to enjoy Hawaii, this place that I've loved for more than half of my life. I need to stop taking things so seriously, like being perfect, and I need to get serious about other things that are more important, like being human.

I'm not superwoman. I'm Wander Woman.

Once you've gone too far, it's hard not to go all the way.
It takes a village to live alone in the rainforest.

12/1/16

Two pieces of good news about the atrocious rumble I heard during last night's dark and stormy...

- It wasn't a granddaddy wild pig.
- The gypsy wagon is still plumb. Meaning, I'm not going to roll off the blocks and into the crater.

The somewhat terrifying news is the crater I'm perched over is bigger than it was yesterday.

One year ago, today, I was deliriously happy and full of optimism. I saw all of this as an adventure. All surmountable and navigable. I envisioned a community who shared in my optimism, confident that when we put our minds to it that nothing would prove impossible.

I still believe this. I've done things much more difficult than this. Pretty much everything I've ever done, I've been told couldn't be done, or that I wasn't the one who could do it.

What's next. I'll cry a lot, it seems. My tears will be interspersed with humor at my own expense, and more of that delirious optimism. Hopefully those fleeting moments of happy will stretch back into occupying my hours, days and weeks.

Eventually the rain will stop. I may or may not topple into the crater before then.

The beginnings of my DIY lava rock driveway.

I'll build my driveway one lava stone at a time.

I'll find people who will help me to create my *Swiss Family Robinson* village.

Until then I'll snuggle Lily, wear fuzzy socks, keep a tea light going at night to make me feel safe from bugs, and, like Dory, I'll just keep swimming.

8/20/19

Now, almost three years later, it's all gone. I'm sitting in the high desert in New Mexico in my RV, wondering what happened, how can it all be gone, and what's next. The answer is the same as it was then, as it always will be with me.

I will intersperse my tears with humor. Fleeting moments of happy will become more than fleeting and ease me into whatever my new life will be. My new normal.

At least that's my hope.

I'm in limbo. Too much got wiped out at once for there not to be an expanse of emptiness on the backside. I'm not unhappy or happy. I'm in between. Writing while I wait. Writing my way back in.

CHAPTER 9:
The Dream That's Been Dreaming Me

1/29/17

Made a run to the Transfer Station. Transfer station. That sounds mysterious and sci-fi... (beam me up, Scotty) like a curiosity and somehow more than what it is. Which is—the dump. As we live on lava with very little dirt, our rubbish goes into shipping containers, and then it gets transferred. I don't know where. Hence, the elegantly utilitarian name.

I'm back in the wagon. We checked it out in the afternoon and the odd smell seemed gone and so safe to sleep in. It's back now. A nighttime-only mold smell? Trying to not get all bunched up around this. It's only until the 8th when I'll be house-sitting again. Ten days.

My 53rd birthday is in six days.

A year ago, today, I posted about how happy I was. Happy as if I was in my right mind, were my exact words. That was before I went on this live-in-the-rainforest-alone-in-a-gypsy-wagon-overlooking-a-50-foot crater-insanely-questionable-yet-unavoidable-vision quest. I had such momentum then that all I could see was a rosy future of miracles and synchronicities.

Ha.

Apparently, this dream that's been dreaming me into being for three decades felt I needed to go that extra steep step of total ego annihilation. Instead of the glamping-ecotourism-village-deep-dive-retreat that I envisioned I'd be living inside of by now, the flesh has been stripped from my bones so I could hang, spinning in the wind. Humbling. Crushing. I love my gypsy wagon.

My friends are holding my vision with me now. Hale Ōhana Honua. The name my land gave to itself. Home for Earth Family. Family. Not individual. And today I was told I had to go through this if I was to fulfill that part of the vision which I wouldn't otherwise be qualified to guide others upon.

Jungle life is raw. And wild. And stark raving, straight-jacket enthralling.

You can't look away. You can't distract yourself with binge TV, (minimal power, zero Wi-Fi), or food grazing (no fridge), so at the end of the day it's all about you, and the coquis, and the wood rats chewing through screens to eat your peanut butter while you sleep. It's about the 20 or so cockroaches who are hitching a ride around town in the trunk of your car, and the crashing of black pigs outside your door. It's about the wind knocking down hundred-foot-tall trees, and it's about them barely missing the roof over your head. It's about 12 inches of rain in a day. It's about perfect sunsets, and the magic of a river of lava flowing into the sea just a few miles away. It's about black sand beaches where dolphins and turtles swim, and the coconut palms and the avocados, and the moon bows, and the mud.

You can run but you can't hide.

I've felt great joy and experienced withering defeats. But I'm in. Like. All. In. Maybe someday I'll write a book that explains why.

Is this ground zero? Hell, if I know. I hope so. I've got shit to do. Like make more dump runs. I mean, more trips to the Transfer Station.

> *Ever have that moment in your sundress when you realize*
> *one more step and you're gonna lose your underwear?*
> *Yeah. Me neither.*

3/17/17

OMG. I hate them. Red ants. Hate.

It began around 2 a.m., night before last. I got stung on the chin. I'm told it's their urine being secreted on your skin that causes the pain. Not an actual bite. Nice.

I sprayed orange oil on all the surfaces before I left in the morning. I sprayed again before going to sleep last night. I dozed off, lulled by the music of the nighttime jungle.

Sharp pain. They're still here. Lights back on: commence with search and destroy.

I found their entry point and, holy cow, we've got swarm. Teeming piles of miniscule torturous specks. All along the window frame of my skylight. You know the one that sits about two and a half feet directly over my head in the loft where I sleep. That's why that one landed on my chin last night. He fell. Or one of his jokester buddies pushed him.

I tore off my pillowcase and put it beneath the window, then grabbed my spray bottle and went to war.

Plop, plop, plop. Writhing blobs of screaming, (I could hear them, I swear) stinging, invasive, little, squirming, dastardly, never-to-sting-anyone-again-after-tonight, red ants, were now dying the true death on my pillowcase. <insert evil laugh here>.

I rolled up the pillowcase and tossed it out into the jungle. Pau. Time to sleep. Lights out. Kitty spoon. Drifting off...and...

I'm itching again. I don't cry. What's the point? I don't get to be the girl in my world. I must be the guy and kill my own bugs. This is so messed up.

It's me or them.

What I did next is what any red-blooded, crazy woman living alone in the jungle, in the middle of the night, in the middle of an infestation, in a 40-year-old WOODEN gypsy wagon would do.

I flicked my Bic.

I lit a bloody fire under their little, red anty butts. I herded them toward the exit. I burnt them to a crisp. I may have singed the wagon and melted some of the silicone around the edging too. In the moment, I didn't care if I burned the wagon down around me.

Now you know. I murder red fire ants. Heartlessly, and with wild abandon. Gleefully and with vengeance.

What a red ant attack looks like.

I've got welts everywhere. Stung beneath both eyes. My left eye is swollen shut.

Afterwards, I fed Lily and laid down to sleep for another half-hour. Once she finished eating, she jumped back into bed with me. And threw up half a can of tuna. I'm up now.

Having a Zen kōan moment...
what is the actual point of Being,
if you're not Doing? Asking for a friend.

3/25/17

"Only to the extent that we expose ourselves over and over to annihilation can that
which is indestructible be found in us."
~Pema Chodron

Somewhere along the way I forgot a lot of important things. Such as, this adventure was my idea. Living off-grid in a tent was my idea. Roughing it, *Robinson Crusoe* style, was my idea. Buying overgrown and uninhabited rainforest a handful of miles from a live volcano, all my idea. All my ideas of grand adventures. Ones that captivated my imagination and made me blind to the challenges which were bigger than any I'd previously attempted.

My unshakable, arrogant, and unreasonable belief that I can do anything my mind can imagine, that's another thing I'd forgotten.

All words of caution fell upon deaf ears. I threw all my eggs into this basket, trusting faithfully that I'd win through on this as I've won through on most other things I've been told couldn't be done. But that I did.

And then it got hard. Just like in all my favorite books. I'd also forgotten that part. The part where they almost give up, right before they win. Right before things happen. Right before the shift. The tipping point. The miracle. I'd forgotten the stages of the Hero's Journey.

I remembered The Beginnings, The Calls. The excitement of something new, Meeting Friends, Allies, and Enemies. Finding Mentors. Then, The Approach, when things go off kilter. All stages in the Hero's Journey. Until finally, they smack you upside the head and hurl you headlong into the Dark Night of the Soul. The existential crisis. The place of no turning back but only going forward because the changes you've experienced are too profound to forget, or to retreat from. You are forever altered and now you must continue on.

Because, intentionally or not, the bridge has been burned.

Because there's been a shipwreck and you must make do, or you will die.

Too bad if you're tired of it. Too bad if it's too hard. Too bad if there are cannibals on their way to eat you. This is it. This is your bag of tricks. The hand you've been dealt. This is your time of tedium when you wonder if this is as good as it's ever going to get, and if, indeed, it is as it feels, and you're going to be stranded here, alone, forever.

You long for the before, even though when you were in it, you were longing for the now, and for the hope and the excited anticipation of the possibility of what's to come.

Because you long to grow. You're compelled. You're not satisfied with the status quo.

You hate not being the expert, the authority, the go-to gal. You hate it, but not quite as much as you love the thrill of the climb, or the passages you traverse on the way to knowing stuff you didn't know before. And you love when you win out to the other side. You love the feeling of triumph of doing what you've been told cannot be done.

You've done this enough to know there is another side. That the dark night doesn't last forever. But you hate the looks people give you, the raised eyebrows, the skepticism regarding your choices, the pity, and the way they question the wisdom of your path.

As if they know.

Because you know that they cannot conceive of what it is you're doing. What they see is the outside, and their perception is shaped by their own stories, fears, or abandoned dreams.

You hate them thinking they have your answers when mostly they don't even have their own. You know that they sit in the comfort of their four walls, treading water, longing for an adventure, but locked into their safety zones, believing that what they have is what you're looking for. They think they know, and you no longer bother to explain because the explanation is more than they want to understand.

I want the win on the outside to match the win on the inside.

To be both an inspiration, and a dire warning. Because no dream comes without its challenges.

It doesn't matter. They can look at me in that patronizing way, thinking they know something that I don't, thinking that if only I'd done it another way, or not at all, that I wouldn't be in this situation.

Full circle back to, I chose this. I chose to take on the jungle and the mud and the bugs and rodents and the wear and tear this takes on everything, from my car, to my belongings, to my relationships, and my health. To the tearing down of my ego and self-worth. Which is the actual point. That's the big win. Self-annihilation.

I chose this existential crisis. This crisis of spirit, psyche, and soul. It's not what most people choose. Why choose to conquer a jungle, when I could just write a book and have a regular home (she says, tongue-in-cheek). Why, in the words of Henry David Thoreau, live out a life of quiet desperation?

I do not know. I look around me and I still don't see my tribe. My compadres. My partners in crime. I now doubt that I ever will. Because I am never satisfied being inside of someone else's dream. My eyes are locked on the horizon, on the what's next, on the what's next to impossible. Which almost always includes a Dark Night of the Soul.

In the Dark Night lurks those things that cracked my heart and broke my soul, leaving pieces of me behind to cry alone in the shadows. This year I have been forced, finally, to speak out loud the true pain of me. The rejection of the victim identification that's driven me to succeed, and to prove I'm a woman who is as strong and brave and capable as a man. Or better.

My choices terrify you. You fear me, or you fear for me. You see me in my anxiety and despair and choose distance, or advise retreat, because you forget, if you ever knew, who I am, and that to me, retreat is not an option. Regrouping, rerouting, being in the bamboo-bending aikido of it all, those are my options.

I hate that I've gone through the weeping and fear and helpless hopelessness. I hate that I've resented my chronic pain and fatigue for their unfairness, both for getting in my way, and for their promise of an acceptable exit excuse if I were so inclined. I hate that I've allowed my ego to back me into this corner of believing I don't have a choice, when always, there's a choice. I want what I want when I want it, and how I want it.

Like, now. I don't know what the other choices are because for each new idea that comes, I've been trying to fit it inside of my original choice.

Maybe the new ideas are too big for that.

I want it all, and I want it now. I own this land. This land is mine.

Just because I can't do it all in one day, just because I've got no running water, just because my car is failing, just because I get migraines, and I get tired after a few minutes, and because everything hurts. Just because I don't have a phone or consistent Wi-Fi, just because my son is ignoring me, just because no one is rushing in to rescue me, just because the red ants and rats and coquis think my pillow is their pillow, doesn't change that this is mine.

Mine. My wagon. My platform. My craters and rifts and lava tubes. My trees and berries and flowers. My street. My neighbors. My orchids, my ferns, my mold. My cockroaches, my rats, my slugs, my pigs, my birds, my mongoose, my geckos, my Lily. My love. My life. Mine.

Break loose from those perceptions that blind and bind. Go ahead and see the world in another way. Forget about not seeing eye to eye with those who've been here longer, or those who've never been here at all. Forget what this looks like to the outside world, because this isn't something that just happened to you. You chose it.

You always choose the awkward way because you know it's the quickest route between two points. It also can be the most treacherous.

You haven't failed. You bought land and chose to live this way because the alternative was to not buy it at all. You took this biggest leap of all because you wanted the grand adventure. And guess what, this is what it looks like along the way. You didn't plan on getting sick. Nobody does. That's only one of the wrenches amongst the multitude of causes of your descent.

Stop feeling sorry for yourself based on what you think others might think of how you're living. It's none of your business what they think of you. They have no idea where you're going. You aren't choosing their destination of safe harbor. You choose the open seas, then long for safe harbor during the typhoon. Safe harbor comes in its own time. But it always comes. You always weather the storm.

This journey shall not be aborted. I see flickers of light filtering into my darkness. I'm having fleeting moments of hope and my faith has begun to stir. There is another side. There's always another side.

This is life. It's the way things are. It's a trajectory. It's physics. This may be the start of my return to the light. My land forced me to get real and to earnestly feel the grief of my life. That's why I've done this. In order to feel whole. I may have done work in the past, but I never went all the way into the hole in my soul. This was my way to become whole.

There's no step toward self-unity that does not include self-annihilation.

Rules only work if we remain in collusion with the illusion.

CHAPTER 10:
Not Easy to Be My Friend

3/29/17

It's not easy being my friend. It's not easy to be friends with someone who, half the time (it seems), is standing on the edge of a cliff and about to dive without wings. It's hard to watch me building the plane on the way down as I fall. It's hard to handle the stress of me stressing.

It's frustrating that what's so clear to you, is not to me. It's frustrating that what makes sense to me makes no sense to you. And it's scary. You want to be safe. You want me to be safe. You want to minimize the risks in your life while I seem to chase them.

You don't want me to hurt because when you love someone, and they hurt, it hurts you. You don't want to get too close because you're afraid you might find yourself taking risks you wish you hadn't.

Guess what. That's on you. Those are your longings and dreams and fears being triggered into life by the mirror you're seeing in my reflection. We do that for each other.

I am a catalyst. I am that person.

Maybe you think if you keep your distance you can't catch what I have, like it's a disease to avoid instead of a symptom of your own evolution.

You can't catch from me what you don't already have.

I don't have the time nor the inclination to parse myself out in bite-size pieces.

Fear is a natural reaction to moving closer to your truth. The courage to die continually.

Fear kicks your ass into being receptive. Stop struggling. When we buy into guilt, we are practicing guilt.

Guilt is a habit of thinking. The more you think about it, the stronger it gets wired into your brain, until finally, it becomes the default option. It becomes the go-to response. We've created this self-conditioned reality through repetition. It's time to stop that practice.

Guilt is a response to feeling we've done something wrong, so the cure to the practice of guilt, is to think of what to do instead. Ten lashes across the psyche won't manifest our desires, but even the slightest of shifts in how we respond the next time can. Feeling guilty tricks us into believing we're absolved of responsibility because our action of choice is to self-chastise, which is no action at all. Changing what we do is our only absolution.

So.

Renounce the tenacious hope that you can be saved from who you really are. Who I really am.

When I was 12, I had this vision. I even wrote it down.

I am a catalyst.

Did I know what that meant? Not even. I knew the word but had no idea what it was going to mean in my life.

Being a catalyst means being a walking tipping point. I catalyze your secret fantasies, or your silent fears and unspoken hopes. I've seen people heal lifelong, ancestral wounds in one 'accidental' conversation with me.

> *My job, or gift, is to show up and*
> *ask you the questions you don't want to answer*
> *but are afraid you'll never be asked.*

If you're reading this, you're likely at a tipping point of your own. You're at the crossroads where whichever direction you choose is going to alter your life in some way. Don't think that by choosing nothing that you haven't chosen. You have. By default.

I choose to choose. I choose to take risks that others look at sideways. I'm driven to know what's around the next bend, or in that pile of boulders in the field, or down the ravine, or hidden deep inside the rainforest. Or deep inside of me. Sometimes it works out, and sometimes I'm left wondering why I chose to do this. And then I wonder something simpler, that I forget to think of when things are going my way, which is, where's the love of my life who could be here right now, kissing my forehead and making me laugh and saying to me, "It'll be okay, Punkin'."

4/8/17

We hold ourselves together through the habit of our opinions. We are not our opinions and ideas, but we believe that we are. Rarely do we recognize that we are only figments of our own imagination.

Questioning what we believe leads to the obliteration of the ways in which we aren't being authentic. You are not your persona. A persona is a façade, a made-up creation, based on who we think we need to be to impress, fit in, rebel, or whatever it is about ourselves that takes work to maintain. Work we're not necessarily aware of until we get so tired of holding it up, that we drop it. That's when we begin to stop being figments of our own imagination.

Instead of beating myself up, I can lean into this unknown and allow myself to expand.

Having no ground to stand on is a remarkable stroke of luck. The trick is allowing it to be what causes us to soften and inspire us, instead of curling inward.

Discard right and wrong and relax upon the groundlessness.

- No more struggle - meditation is how we stop fighting ourselves and struggling with circumstances. Stop calling it the enemy.
- Using poison as medicine - instead of fighting it, breathe it in. Tonglen. Allow the challenges, or questions, or obstacles to become seeds of compassion and openness.
- Breathe in the storyline instead of rejecting it because it's not what you think it's supposed to be.
- Breathe out big space and freshness.
- See whatever arises as enlightened wisdom – don't pre-judge the epiphanies as they are forming inside of the chaos.
- Lower your standards and relax into what is.
- Totally commit to the experience. Agitation is resistance to sanity.
- Let go of your exit plan.
- Realize your true nature. Are you a fish, or are you a cat?
- Each time you surrender you release resentment, depression, and pride. With each surrender you shed more of your habitual, ancestral baggage.
- Take refuge in your warriorship, your leaps of faith, and intentionally breaching your safety zones.
- Congratulations.

Most of all, suspend your disbelief. Because no matter how much you know, or think you know. You don't.

CHAPTER 11:
Homestead

4/15/17

Fish don't ride bicycles and gypsy psychologists/coaches don't homestead.

This doesn't mean a fish can't be taken on a bike ride, or that a Wander Woman brainiac can't participate in a homesteading project. It's just that in neither case is peddling their forte.

I think it's actually brilliant that I figured this out in under two years. And it's amazing how much has been accomplished in spite of my ineptitude, and my disinclination toward peddling in the first place. Gypsy mermaids don't ride bicycles. Unicorns or seahorses, yes. Bicycles. no.

Clearly, had I looked at the work I've succeeded at in the past, and pondered how, if at all, to apply that information to my current situation, I'd have seen the error of my ways long ago, and with far more clarity. My strengths lie elsewhere. This isn't judgment. This is clarity. Like a fish recognizing it's not a cat and jumping back into the water before it dies of suffocation.

In the past, my greatest successes have occurred when I worked for organizations that were stumbling, usually due to either rapid growth or long-term stagnation. In other words, someone was already peddling, however haphazardly, when I jumped onto the banana seat.

In every instance, I began by observing. Eventually the form in their chaos would emerge and we would proceed accordingly.

I take the necessary time to allow the chaos to swirl around in order to become acquainted with what is already there. Out of this, organically evolves the curriculum or systems and procedure manuals that get things on course.

I'm not interested in sticking around afterwards for the daily grind of it all. Once the chaos gets in order my energy is fired up. My brain says it's time to peddle faster, peddle more, peddle bigger, and peddle better, and do it NOW. Which freaks them out. They've barely gotten used to reaching their current goals and are nowhere near ready for the ones I foresee.

No wonder they think I want control. In my mind, I'm following a natural course of events, according to the patterns I've identified in their own chaos, but they can't see it yet. I've found it's best to make a quick exit rather than stick around and become the fallout victim for the panic that comes as their dream rolls on out of their control.

In the case of Corey of the Jungle, I've been doing this bassackwards. I've had to learn on my feet how to listen for the form in my own chaos, something I've never been patient enough to do. In place of patience, I've been pretending I'm something I'm not.

Just the word "homestead." Home. Stead. Steady. Home. Ha!

My words are more like — tiara, adventure, and glitter.

None of this is super new news to you or me. But how many of us know things, Truths, with a capital "T" about ourselves, that we:

1. Ignore.
2. Never allow to go any further than our brains.

In other words, how often do we do something with an epiphany besides go, "aha!" and continue as we already have been? How often does it cause us to veer that one percent that makes all the difference in our destination?

I bring this up now because someone just asked to buy my land. Cash. At a profit.

This project has been the hardest thing I've ever done, which is saying something because I've done some pretty tough stuff in my life.

Do I give up now? Would it be giving up, or would I be conceding to my lack of qualifications for something so tremendously beyond my scope of abilities?

It's tempting. I could take that money and travel again. Or get that teardrop trailer.

But in the end, it would mean I no longer had my land. This magical place of transformation that has challenged me to grow bigger, better, and stronger more quickly than any experience before.

I want to say "yes" to escape the difficulties. And I want to say "no" because believing this is the only way out of the challenges is rooted in scarcity. As if this is the only way I can learn this particular thing, and there aren't dozens of other, less taxing, less painful ways.

What I don't want to do is continue to face any of it as a fish from the banana seat of a bicycle. I'm more of a cat. In a tree. Chasing butterflies.

Perception is a mirror, not a fact.

4/9/17

Please come for me. Please hold me. Please love me. Please tell me I matter and you're sorry and you love me more than anything and it's all going to be okay. That you're going to put your arms around me and fill the void in my soul. Tell me there's a reason to hope because you're here now and always will be.

Don't let me sob alone until all that's left is that gasping ache where my heart was. Before I knew you didn't care. That I wasn't worth fighting for. That I wasn't good enough to be loved.

I cried. I cried. I cried because any minute now you'd come. But you didn't. Ever. Until I finally knew you never would. Until I gave up hoping. Because I don't matter enough to fight for. I'm dispensable.

Entertaining, inspiring, but not someone to keep.

You didn't fight to protect me. Or stand up for me. You didn't say, no more, you will not harm her because she's that important to me. I cherish her. I love her beyond all reason, simply because.

I say it to me now. I matter.

No one said, I will seek you out, I will check on you. I need to know you're okay. I will want you until you know without a doubt that you are not alone. I will never leave.

I say it to me now. I'm worth protecting.

I didn't know. That I could do this for myself. Or that it would be enough. I thought if I stopped waiting for someone to show up, and instead took their place and stood for myself, that then no one would ever show up. It's hard to let go of wanting someone to lean on. Hard. Not impossible, and when I was able to do it, the world didn't end.

When I surrendered. When I let go of needing your shoulder and accepted my own instead, it ended. That wound in my soul that went so deep that no human being could ever hope to fill it for another.

I chose to not waste the awful ache that was caused by every phase of my living in the jungle, or by the silence of my family, or the treachery of their deceit.

I used it. I used it to access places in myself that were otherwise unavailable. I dove into my own abandonment. No one would choose to hurt so deeply on purpose, but in order to heal a wound so old that you no longer know it exists outside of yourself, you must go there. Otherwise you are accustomed to it, and you think it's who you are, like your skin and your heart are who you are. It's not. You are more than a sum of the parts you were given.

It took these brutal woundings for me to see that I didn't deserve any of the wounds that came before.

Trauma is a terrible gift. Don't squander it. Use that shit.

Be empowered by your words. Not disassembled.

4/9/17

It's taken me over two years to feel, in my bones, what once came to me naturally: I'm home. In Hawaii. Where I've felt I belonged since my first trip to the islands in 1981.

For 35 years, off and on, I've lived or worked across this chain of islands, and still I've managed to pick up some of the bad habits of mainland living, namely, stress, competitiveness, and the drive to overachieve. It's for these very reasons that most people who move to Hawaii, end up leaving. The habits are misunderstood. They aren't who we are, just who we've been told we're supposed to be. We have become our habits. Who are we without them?

We think we want to go with the flow, to live the pace of Hawaiian time, and to do without the high pressure living that we claim to hate. What we don't get, what we may never get, is that even the lifestyles we claim to detest are our addictions.

What do you do with yourself without the distractions of thousands of choices? Where to go, who to see, what to do, what to wear; when the parameters are a microcosm of what we resent and dislike?

The entry price for paradise? Giving up who you thought you were. Finding out your current storyline is but one of the many possible You's. Becoming comfortable being neither here nor there but being right where you find yourself.

Not everyone chooses to go through the extremes of off-grid living alone in the rainforest. You may even comfort yourself with "yeah, I wouldn't do it that way, so I won't have those experiences." That's a false premise. A false hope.

No matter how you choose to live, and if you intend to stay, the islands will make demands upon you that will be unique.

I think I sprained my thumb. In paradise.
I think I'm gonna say that after everything. In paradise.

CHAPTER 12:
Chronic Illness

5/6/17

Not much to say, or not wanting to say much. Shrug.

On the almost eve of my upcoming visit to California, one filled with the promise of adventure, and catching up with my besties, I have a confession.

Anxiety. A lovely byproduct of my ever so random medical conditions of chronic fatigue and polymyalgia rheumatica. In response, I've developed this new coping habit which arose spontaneously one morning. I'd barely begun to wake up before I felt the dread in the pit of my stomach, and for no good reason. I vehemently growled out, "Nooooooooooo!! Just NO!"

Seriously. I growled. I growl.

The first time this happened, I surprised myself. I didn't know it was coming. I was angry! I don't get anxious, I'm Wander Woman! I'm fearless and strong. Dammit!

It worked, at least long enough to get me out of bed and into my day.

It gets my fight on. It gets Lily fed, it gets my supplements and meds down my gullet, and it gets me into my car and out into the sunshine.

Living with chronic illness and pain is no joke. It's also not something I often share. I'm one of those people who's heard, "You don't look sick," enough times that it's easier to keep the reality of it to myself, as I've done for years. Plus, I'm still in denial...you know, if I pretend it ain't so, it ain't so. Riiiiight.

It's real. And it sucks. And being anxious embarrasses me. It makes me feel weak. It cramps my style. When I don't show up to something, I prefer you think I'm a flake, rather than you know I am sick. In my mind, being sick is being weak. Plus, I've got other plans. Plans which do not include limitations, or the isolation I've mastered after years of practice. I was so good at it even I didn't know I was doing it. At least until now, when I've created a situation that doesn't allow for much hiding.

Sometimes a condition is a message about letting go, or getting on track, or pointing yourself in another direction, or it's about surrender. Sometimes it's all these and more. And, as Freud says, sometimes a cigar is just a cigar. Even medical intuitive, Carolyn Myss, says that finding out the cause doesn't go hand in hand with the cure.

I've blamed myself, and I've been judged by others. I've wondered if my body is reflecting the damage I feel in my soul. Or am I reflecting my untamed jungle? As far as I'm concerned, at this point, we can all shut up about it, because sometimes shit works in our favor, and sometimes we don't know what our favor is until after the fact.

I've done all the airy fairy, woo-woo, spiritually evolved, magical thinking, rain dancing, positivistic rituals I could think of or been told to try. I've written things down and burned them in coconut bowls and fiery incense. I've done the affirmations. I've thanked my conditions. I've dialogued with shame and self-blame. I've leaned into them. I've surrendered to them. I've faked it 'til I maked it. Except I didn't. I'm not better yet. As far as I'm concerned, my taking the blame is nothing short of spiritual narcissism, as if I know more about the best outcomes than powers greater than myself know.

I've also got this big, analytical brain, chock-full of education in psychology and decades of experience in the field. My brain thinks it can think itself into wellness. That maybe, just maybe, if I was zen enough that I would be well.

I meditate, I write, I don't wallow. I see friends, I laugh, I swim in the ocean, and I soak up the sun. I eat fruits and vegetables picked ripe from the vine. I eat fresh fish. I don't eat fast food or processed crap. I do research. I listen to Buddhist teacher, Pema Chodron. And still, I am not well. Not yet. Not zen enough.

In the end, being sick is not my fault. It's not about being zen, or enlightened. It's not about this one treatment, or the law of attraction, or NLP, or energy clearing. I've done them all, and more. It's not about 'thinking' myself well. Yoga and essential oils have not cured me.

It's not about completing one side of the Rubik's Cube, or all the sides of the cube. It's about continuing to play the game, even when, no matter what you do, you can't get that one blue square out of the center of the yellow side. It's about growling, "Noooooo!" if that's what it takes to get up and out of bed. It's about getting on with your day, blue square and all. No matter what.

I accept that this is my now. I believe there will someday be a different now. And, this may be as good as it gets.

Apparently, I did have a few things I didn't want to say that needed saying.

7/28/17

Here's what's up. I accepted an offer to be Camp Director at Far Horizons Theosophical Camp, in King's Canyon. It's a volunteer position, and I accepted because it's very light duties. Usually. LOL.

I've been sick since I arrived, the usual chronic fatigue and polymyalgia symptoms exacerbated by an altitude of over 7,000 feet. I couldn't get off the couch the first two days and was about to give up on staying when I was reassured that if I could at least answer phones that would be enough.

I'm slightly better after 10 days. Some days I can walk the 20 feet between my cabin and the kitchen without using my cane. Other days I'm grey, and panting, by the time I open the cabin door. These are the conditions that changed me from who I was to who I now am. The me who I've been grieving for two years. And why I've been deeply depressed and feeling useless, because I can no longer do what I once did.

And. There are no coincidences, only synchronicities. The challenges here at a mostly volunteer camp for small events, like meditation and yoga, are the exact things I'm good at. Finding the form in the chaos. Creating systems. Coaching people.

Except I've discovered I really am sick. There's no denying the contrast between my stamina a few years ago, and now. One conversation and I must lie down afterwards. Two and I have to lie down all the next day.

But I'm still in here. I remember who I am. People still gather in my room, tell me I need to write it all down, tell me people need to hear what I have to say.

I've found I'm still useful, still somewhat larger than life, and still respected for what I can do, even if I have to lie down while doing it, and can only do it for a short time, and within a 20-foot radius.

8/21/17

In the last month I had the opportunity to remember who I was before I got sick. I found that I can still be useful. That I have gifts and life experiences that are unique to me and can be helpful to others when I share them. I got a renewed lease on life. I got hope.

Thank goodness for this experience, because when I came back down the mountain it was to the absolute betrayal of someone I love. And to the turned backs of the family who drew their wagons around him. I'll survive. Always have. But I wish this was one test I could have skipped. My heart seems to be made of stronger stuff than I've given it credit for.

Did life know this was coming, and that without the recent reminder of who I still am, that I likely would not have survived it?

Hope is the magic elixir. Without it, the smallest thing can take you out. With it, you can survive the worst.

I may have been sucker punched but I'm still standing. I'll go back to my jungle and go on with my life. Where there was darkness there is light again.

I'll love you forever. Even now.
More than ever.

9/4/17

I was just told that no one wants to be around someone who's sad. That I need to move on. That my sadness is pitiful. That I am pitiful. Then I turn around and see posts on social media that say someone is listening. I say "bullshit!" when I see that.

I understand. I do. It hurts to see someone you love hurting.

I am moving through. At the pace my body is setting. Not to wallow, but to feel it all the way, so when I do move on, it's real, not just silently eating away at me in order to not be an inconvenience to anyone.

In the meantime, I will pretend I'm okay when those people who think that my sadness is pitiful, that I am pitiful, who call up their friends who I don't even know to say I'm pitiful, are near. I won't take it personally that there are people I love who are choosing not to show up at all. Who say there are two sides to every story and are in disbelief when I say, not this time. I will lean into the pain of once again, not being believed. I will cry alone. And I will make it. I'm pretty sure I'll make it. I choose to not make this all worse by believing the worst. It's bad enough on its own.

Remember this. Please. The next time someone tells you that someone they know has committed suicide, and they are wondering why they didn't say something, know that this could be why.

Because we can tell by a gesture, or the roll of your eyes, or the type of questions you ask, or comparisons, or your energetic recoil, or by your silence when we speak, that you don't want to hear about it. That your own silent pain is too great to be capable of being present for us. That no one has given your pain the room it needed, so there can't possibly be room for someone else's.

Or, we can stop living in that kind of scarcity. As if there is only so much love to go around. Instead we can decide that we need to show up for each other, beyond a cut and paste, or a "like" on social media, even when it sucks. Even when it's hard.

I'm not chastising you or begging for attention. And I'm speaking for more than just me.

I'm speaking for everyone who feels alone. Our friends who believe it when someone says they are pitiful, and they feel ashamed. The people we love, who believe that they are a burden if they dare to relinquish the fallacy of positivity. The ones who right now, are feeling the terribleness that tempts them to leave the planet, a temptation that might one day win.

They need you to talk to them, listen to them, tough love them into fighting through the feelings, and to remind them, with your presence, with your gaze, that they aren't alone. That they matter. When they are so sad it hurts to look at them, look harder. This is how they might get through.

People survive because we look at them, and we see them when they can't see themselves. We remind them of who they are when they've forgotten.

There are days when what it felt right to write yesterday
feels like I said too much today.

9/5/17

I don't matter.

No amount of visits from friends going out of their way to see me and bring gifts or take me out changes the fact that I'm nothing.

I do nothing. I contribute nothing. I'm treading water in my own life, going nowhere.

For years now. Doing nothing. I can't work, I can't have hobbies that involve doing anything. I do nothing because it's all I can do. So, I am nothing. I have no sense of purpose, no reason. My son gave me purpose and reason, but now he's grown. He's gone. He doesn't need me. I'm nothing.

Even if I just had an easier place to invite people to come to. If I had a cleaner kitchen to prepare potluck meals. A place to be on my computer and to write. If Raj hadn't totaled the Miata while I was in California and had fixed it, as promised. Anything.

But I'm nothing. I was something. What happened? Please god, help me with these things, gently. I'm tired. I need a miracle. I'm leaning into the arms of my guides and guardian angels this time. I hurt with heartache and sadness.

It's my absent son. My narcissistic family. It's my health. I've lost my reason. I feel like I've lost my love because it's been wrapped up in him. He was the sun that I revolved around. Now I've lost my orbit; I'm spinning through space. Ricocheting. Careening from one hard edge to the next like a pinball.

I want to learn to control who can walk into my dreams and make me cry.

Please bring love into my heart again. Bring me someone or something to love, something that is mine. Loving deeply gives me a sense of purpose. I can't survive without it. You gave me my son, and that saved my life. Somehow, I need this to happen again. A partner, or a project, or a mission that I can spontaneously give my heart and soul to.

Love will save my life.

9/9/17

I write about my experiences because I can.
If I was a carpenter, I might hammer nails to work it out.
If I was an actor, I might pour my emotions into my next role.
I'm not. I write. I share what I learn because I was given a gift,
one that I've spent my life practicing, so that what I learn I can share with others.

I believe we don't always have to learn the hard way. But it is the fastest.

Sometimes life reads like a book, as if we've planned things to line up thus and so. Talk to most writers though and they'll tell you that they haven't planned those things any more than we're able to predict what happens in real life. Foreshadowing happens without any help from us.

Stories take on lives of their own, even the stories that we think are ours. This is where chaos happens, when, out of all the scenarios that could occur, the ones that do occur are the ones that line up to change our lives. It's more than fate, it's kismet, written in the stars, like the woman I saw in the stars so long ago on Maui. The place we were going before we knew of its existence.

Coming to the Big Island was inevitable. All the time that I was elsewhere, doing other things, I knew I was putting it off. I didn't know what was waiting for me, I assumed, wrongly, that it would be as it had been on the other islands, in other times, and that it was my retirement. My time to rest. Which is probably why I put it off for so long. I wasn't ready to rest.

Ha. Some rest. More like an interlude. A veer from the path I'd been on. Because veering is all we need to do when we want our lives to change. We think when we want big changes, we must make big changes. Not true. We just need to veer. Like an airplane. They can't make abrupt right or left turns, but over time, taking just a 1% veer can mean the difference between landing in Dubai or Siberia.

Getting sick has forced me to stay, and to endure things, and to learn my way through them. I was forced to veer. When I scream into the jungle, what do you want from me, and I hear back things like, go to the pond, I have to surrender. I don't always understand. It made no sense to me that by floating in the pond I was going to meet who I met and do the things I did. I made friends, and it was healing to float, to just be. I learned about truly grieving. Truly feeling powerless. Truly resting in a world where I'd spent all my years proving. Never resting. Never being satisfied. Never being okay. Never holding still long enough to become a part of something.

I fought it. Hard. And then I didn't. Someone asked me if I could do anything for the rest of my life what would it be? I'd go to school, I'd write, and I'd work on my tan.

I look around me. It doesn't match what I saw in my head, but it's close enough.

I check out a dozen books from the library every week, studying whatever intrigues me, be it Pema Chodron and Buddhism or epigenetics or solar power. And I am always immersed in something science fiction, the writing of visionaries who open up worlds of possibilities.

I write essays and post them on Facebook or tuck them away if I'm not ready to have that conversation.

And every day I am at the pond.

Studying. Writing. Working on my tan.

I didn't plan things this way. I thought of it, I wanted it, and this is how it showed up. I must pay better attention. I could have missed it.

CHAPTER 13:
Truth Telling

9/10/17

I've made most of the Facebook posts I've written since August 20th private. I haven't deleted them, but I don't think it's relevant for them to remain public. They've served their purpose.

I did that once. Deleted all I had written. I was 17. I walked in on my mother reading my journals. She told me I should burn them. So, I did.

What was so bad that had to be burned? Raw emotion? Anger? Pain? My real life in that awful house with those terrible people. Of course. I wrote about what I wasn't supposed to talk about. My memories of those years became sketchy, as if my brain erased them at the moment they were burned from the paper.

I do remember those were my angry years. I was telling. About incest and rape and violence and humiliation. I would run away, to my Grandma Cherole. I said she was more of a mother to me. My punishment for that was to not have her anymore. To not be allowed to see her, or to talk to her on the phone. I was told our problems were her fault. I didn't believe that. But. I wanted them to love me. I didn't understand. There was so much to know that I wouldn't know for another 30 years. I chose to believe and allowed them to drive a wedge between us.

I pushed my Gram away. I was mean to her, to the woman who'd given me the most. The most love. The most encouragement. The most support and inspiration and acceptance. The source of my wisdom. The only one who touched me kindly. I believed if I did this, that the rest of them would want me. That I would belong. That they'd realize I was a good person. Not bad.

I was wrong. I can never be good in their eyes because they'd have to rewrite their own histories. And they've passed the lies on to the generations who came after.

Before I could realize my mistake, her heart stopped. She died before I got to say, "I'm sorry. I love you. I got the best of me from you. You saved my life."

11/11/17

When I was 21, I began a journey of healing, and processing, and understanding. My first step was to move away from home, from the Bay Area in Northern California, to San Diego. The next came one evening when I was crying, and my friend asked, "Do you think the way you feel about yourself has anything to do with the way your parents treated you as a child?" I was like, um, NO. Duh.

You see, I knew they were messed up, but I also 'knew' I was broken, irreparably.

That was my moment. He had asked me the question that I didn't know I needed to hear but am so grateful that he asked. Those were the words that shifted what I was looking at. I was unlocked by a question, and that's how it began. It led to my discovering that I'm not broken. I'm not violent. I'm not selfish. I'm not any of what they said, or what I was taught to believe.

I learned that in my efforts to prove I was a good person, I've become an even better one. I've also learned that they will NEVER see this.

Three years ago, a few years after completing graduate school, I moved to Hawaii. I bought an acre of rainforest. To them, my history as I told it was still a lie. I was still 'doomed,' and my degrees were still questionable. And they were contacting my friends to say that, while I might seem okay, if people really knew me, they'd see the truth.

Which begs the question, if my relatives really knew me would they see the truth? And, whose truth? Theirs is the one that protects them from their own shame for failing to keep me safe.

Once upon a time I felt ashamed of what they said about me. Afraid that if it was even 1% true, other people would agree with them. I was afraid to defend myself because they would accuse me of being angry, of having a chip on my shoulder. They'd taunt me, saying that I think I'm smarter than them. Great mechanisms for control, now that I think about it.

I've told myself a bazillion times that I no longer had anything to prove to them. While it was true, I hadn't stopped trying.

Then, two months ago, my son, my heart, joined their ranks. There was no fight. No disagreement. No harsh words. Just total betrayal. And they opened their arms to receive him. It was brutal. I was suicidal. I was in so much pain that I knew I couldn't be alone. I wasn't rational. I was afraid I might do something I couldn't take back.

I wrenched my gaze away from the pain and tried to look for the gift. For the lessons, because it's what I've learned to do in order to survive the insanity. I didn't ask for the pain, but I've learned to not waste it. I can stay a victim, or I can call the pain a gift and find the usefulness in it. What my son did gave me an understanding of my history, that I do not think I could have gotten, like down into my bones, and into my soul, in any other way.

I think that the shattering of my heart set me free.

There are moments in our lives when we reach a crossroads,
when we have to decide whether we are willing to risk
appearing the fool by trying something new, or when we
allow our fears to win by giving up, growing old, and
fading into obscurity without ever experiencing our true purpose.
These are precious moments when our life force and vitality are hanging in the balance.

11/17/17

I haven't posted in a while because nothing's been happening for a while. As we approach Phase Three of Corey of the Jungle, I thought I'd put up a wee post to mark the next threshold moment.

Phase One was about adventure, and discovery. It was full of hope and possibility. It was about miracles and Menehune.

Phase Two was about two steps forward, one step back. It was about the onset of a different reality. It was about grieving the loss of my health and of the me I had been. It was about helping hands, and disappointments. It was about friendship.

Phase Three is about new beginnings after painful losses. It's about a clean slate. A new foundation. It's about recognizing that I'm not a farmer. I'm a vision holder, a guide, a planner, and a writer. It's about discovering what I can do instead of grieving the things I can't. It's about slowing down and allowing the miracles.

My Aunt Jill arrives in a few weeks. She's coming to meet my land, and see what we can see together, anticipating her forthcoming move to the Big Island, and what we will build on it together.

Two years ago this month, I went into escrow.
Deliriously happy, and oblivious to the challenges to come.
My ego has taken a brutal onslaught, and I've been broken down,
broken open, humbled, and seasoned. Sometimes I wish
I'd taken that money and just traveled the world 'til it was spent.
Would I have learned what I have learned? Am I glad I've learned
these things? Glad? No. Grateful? Yes. Now I'm ready for something
peaceful, graceful, gentle, stable, supportive, and kind.

3/18/17

I was raised to be a homeless drug addict. Those were the tools for living that I was given. Not intentionally but by default.

You're tired.

Tired of proving you can do anything a man can do.

Tired of proving yourself at all.

Do you even want to write a book? If you did, wouldn't you have done it by now?

You've proven you can do almost anything someone tells you cannot be done.

You can raise your son into a healthy, productive adult. You can do this while finishing 12 years of college, going from GED to PhD, working full time, and homeschooling him through middle school.

You can travel through six states in an RV, alone, with your cat, Lily. You can dismantle an RV engine, down to the carburetor, with your Swiss Army knife, needle nose pliers, a rubber mallet, and your iPhone.

You can interview Walter Cronkite for an NPR documentary, as an undergraduate, when they said it couldn't be done. You can speak in front of a live audience of 17,000 people and love it.

You can be crew and first mate on Windjammer, a 68-foot schooner, even when the owner says to your face that women are second-rate crew. You can move to Hawaii when you're 22, with a backpack and a bike with two flat tires. No Google. You can learn to hitchhike.

At the helm of Windjammer out of Maui Harbor circa 1987.

You can be published, and interviewed on radio and TV, and your interviews can be printed in languages you don't understand.

You can help new and failing businesses thrive.

You can have a summer affair with the Golden Gate Bridge. You can depart upon an unguided shamanic descent with Fire, and return.

> *You can ask the questions they don't want to answer*
> *but are afraid they'll never be asked.*

You can pick yourself up after being raped by five boys you went to school with. You can go back to that school two days later and survive being called a slut. You can survive being pressured to drop the charges, so you don't ruin their lives.

You can stand up to your dad when he says he's 99% sure you're telling him the truth about the things he's done to you but denies remembering because he was drunk. You can tell him when he says that, that he's calling you a liar. And he can surprise you by saying you're right.

I believe you.

You can spend 30 years of your life healing from the trauma of childhood abuse, neglect, and humiliation. You can be strong enough to finally end relationships, putting a stop to the toxicity and delusional narcissism.

You can defend yourself in court, and win.

You can grow up being rejected by aunts and uncles because they believed your parents' lies. You are a teller. You told on them. So, they said you lied. You can say you lied about it all when your parents tell you if you don't, you'll ruin everyone's lives.

Your Truth becomes the scapegoat for ruining other people's lives.

You can grow up under the cloud of being an illegitimate baby, forced upon your mother. Someday, you can stop wondering about the family who was on their way to the hospital to adopt you, after spending the first two days of your life on the planet shrouded in the hospital nursery. You can stop wondering why your mother suddenly decided to keep you, then reject you, and later admit how grateful she was when your dad came after you instead of her.

You can think on your feet when your boyfriend bends your neck further than you thought possible, punching you, telling you he's going to take you into a cane field and "get it over with." You can hold it together long enough to pretend to call home about your new boombox, when really you were calling 911 with him standing next to you. You can survive two miscarriages with him. You can leave.

You can buy an acre of voraciously wild rainforest near flowing lava and live on it in a tent without a bathroom.

You can survive living 3,000 miles apart from your son, your heart.

You can survive all the ex-boyfriends and fiancés who couldn't say I love you, or who could, but who loved your free spirit so much they couldn't stop themselves from attempting to diminish you. You can survive being alone.

You can cry and not die.

You can love the young woman you were, who was brave enough to believe she could escape her fate. You can admire her courage and the risks she took in order to keep going, and to find ways to heal.

You can fight for a cause and help it to win. You can stand up for what's right, even when it means you might lose someone by doing so. You can say you're sorry. You can make amends without expectations. You can bare your soul to someone you don't want to ever lose.

You can get up every day and walk through the physical pain, knowing the hole in your soul is because no one in your family knows about these pieces. You can survive not hearing, "Congratulations, you've raised an amazing young man," instead of, "What a surprise this is." Or, "Congratulations on your graduate degrees in psychology." Instead of their validity being publicly questioned. Or, "Wow, you bought land in Hawaii. We'd love to visit."

Crickets

You've proven yourself to be as strong as a man. Now you just want to be a woman. You want a family who is kind to you, loves you, wants to be close to you and know you, and wants to celebrate you.

You're tired of being all the pieces. Playing all the roles. Being on your toes. Citing your references. Like you've just done here. Proving yourself. Wondering why are you the thing to resist?

You haven't traveled enough or done anywhere near as much as you dreamed of doing. You kept going back to them. You kept hearing them in your head, and you kept doing what you wanted but in ways you thought they'd approve. So they'd think you are good. Smart. Worthy. Of value.

You've poured too much energy into that bottomless, meaningless nothingness. They've proven they can say, we're sorry, we didn't know, we'd have done something, and within days revert to the status quo.

You can navigate the paradox of knowing if you give up on your goals now then they can point and say see, we were right all along, we knew you couldn't do it. And if you continue, then you've also failed because they can say see, look at her struggle, it'll never work. She's doomed.

Even though almost everything you've ever set out to accomplish, you've been successful at. And they don't know, or if they do, they don't care. It pisses them off even more. It must be hard to live with your own incongruence.

And then you can learn to live as if no one is watching. To write as if no one is reading. You can lean into not mattering to them, because you matter to yourself. You can stop wondering what would happen if they gave you a second thought. You can stop fearing that if you gave up on them that you'd have nothing left.

Now when you wonder who you are, you know this for what it is; the existential crisis of being human.

This is that tune the runs through everything.

Blank.

There's a glimmer of hope within the wicked emptiness between these words.

You have the ability to live between worlds.
Both daemonic and shamanic,
to blur boundaries and transform them into horizons.

12/6/17

Life teaches you shit. Through that shit, you live or die. You get it, or you get it again.

You have awful moments. You have 'aha' moments, and from them you learn. You gain mastery, you feel more ease. As a matter of fact, you may become so confident that you slip into what may appear to others nothing short of arrogance.

You might even begin to believe that if you can dream it, you can be it. Whatever 'it' may be.

You may believe you can do anything you set your mind to. You may decide to risk appearing the fool, over and over again, in pursuit of something that only you can see. You may decide (gasp) to be your own authority.

Arrogance in service to itself is ego. Arrogance in service to a dream is confidence. It can inspire the level of commitment necessary in order to do the things that others around you say cannot be done. It can also irritate the shit out of people.

That's not your problem.

CHAPTER 14:
Twelve Minutes

1/13/18

We woke up to a Civil Defense alert this morning. It took only a few seconds to feel it all.

In those seconds, I went from disbelief, to acceptance, to relief. The struggle was over. I could go home now. Out of this body, and heart, and mind, out of its pain and suffering and learning and growth. My work here was done. I went outside to the dirt road to watch and to wait. I thought of who I love, and of not getting to say goodbye.

The next alert said we had 12 minutes before the missile arrived. Not enough time to get anywhere in Puna.

For almost an hour we waited for something to happen. After 48 minutes of silence the news finally told us it was a false alarm. Some believe the story that it was a technician's mistake and a faulty dropdown menu. Most of us think that's a lie.

Afterwards, and all day, I was silent and sad. I felt alone. No frantic or concerned calls from loved ones. No goodbye from my son in those 48 minutes of not knowing.

I accept that I've created this life that I'm living. I chose no contact. But I wonder...32 years ago when my journey of processing and understanding began...would I have chosen to take this road less traveled if I knew then how alone I would feel now?

Yes, is still my answer. Because if they can't care when an apparent ballistic missile is heading in my direction, then they certainly can't care on any other day.

What a way to start the year.

This should have been the worst thing that happened to us in 2018. To know that our lives were going to end in 12 minutes, and there was nothing we could do but go into the street to greet it. There was no bomb shelter, or nearby cave to hide inside. We weren't in Honolulu, where people were scrambling to get into the sewers. And for what? What would be left when we emerged? No thanks.

Better to make my peace and shrug it off. I had a good run. I know who cares. I know what matters to me. I'm good with me. And that was the gift I didn't know I'd been given until the lava came.

I already knew what mattered. Those 12 minutes brought a clarity I wouldn't have otherwise had. I knew where things stood. Who was going to show up, or not. I knew who I cared about, and that I could care even if they couldn't.

We knew we were on our own.

I knew that I was.

It was a week into the eruptions before I thought to remember I had a brother and sister, cousins, aunts and uncles, nieces and nephews, and a son who hadn't called to see if I was okay.

Because of those 12 minutes on January 13th, it hadn't occurred to me to think of them. Or to miss them or to feel alone. I felt whole. I knew who I could count on, and they were around me. In this bizarre way, those 12 minutes had done what I hadn't been able to do on my own. Without knowing it, I'd let go. For real. I'd shifted my gaze from looking toward them, to being present.

The lava finished what the ballistic missile began. With a few exceptions, my time with my relatives is done. Complete. Whatever contracts we came into this lifetime with, are fulfilled. Or nullified. Which is another book.

4/28/18

Time and again I come up against the fiery wall of pain that is made up of the lies and betrayals of the someones I trusted. Because it doesn't stop. Because I keep forgetting it's just who they are. And before you jump in to school me, no one needs to tell me I am the thoughts I choose. I get it.

What most don't get, or admit is, letting go of people who are supposed to care about us is easier said than done. I don't write about my experiences because I think that my pain and losses are any bigger, or deeper, or more wounding than anyone else's. That's not the point.

I write because I can. Some can't.

I don't walk in your shoes, nor do you walk in mine. Therefore, I won't tell you what, or how to feel. Or to not feel. Or when to move on. Or to just let go. In return, I expect the same.

Of course, you'll do as you please, just know that to give advice, without first seeking permission, or finding out if your advice is desired, or even pertinent, is patronizing, an assumption, and more for your ears and ego, than it is for mine. Don't forget that goofy little saying, when you point one finger at me, that there are three fingers pointing directly back at you.

What this comes down to, for me, is of a spiritual nature. After decades of accessing, experiencing, and utilizing a vast range of modalities, trainings, and educational materials, and finding exponential relief, the wall still looms. Not all the time. Sometimes. Because my human self is still trying to make sense of things that are senseless.

I keep hoping for the relief of being immersed in a project, or a relationship, something to distract me from how much it hurts. But so far, having a project hasn't been enough.

Rather than give in, which is different from surrender, or give up, which is death, I am choosing to deepen my spiritual practice, as well as my writing practice. Which is to lean in.

I think any other choice is a waste of some perfectly awful experiences.

Bring on the alchemy.

You're not made for blueprints. You're made for trail blazing.
You're meant to throw caution to the wind. You're meant to fall,
and to fail, and you're meant to do the things you're told are impossible.

CHAPTER 15:
Epic Life

2/22/18

I'm having an epic life.

It's the little things that make it so.

Hot potato with bacon soup, fresh from Island Naturals. Soft blankets. Coquis 'coqui'ing' out the open side door. Rain in my jungle.

Friends dropping by unannounced.

Walking around my place with them, imagining the things to come in Phase Three of Corey of the Jungle. Invitations to stay in dry places with hot tubs. Hot tea neighbor walking over to share a tomato beer, and Peter Gabriel on his headphones, before heading back to his place to continue dancing in the rain.

My god. Living simply, is simply living.

What happened with my family last summer was scorching. It hurt so bad I wanted to die. It was an awful gift. And somehow, I was able to not waste it, but to use it to go into the darkest of my dark places.

To be the archeologist to my history.

To go into such inky blackness, sensing that only such a dreadful anguish could allow my entry into this older, other, most devastating sorrow. Knowing that in no other way might I have been able to access it, and to heal. Because no one in their right mind would consciously choose to go to a place they weren't sure they could survive.

There is no final, final. It's not over 'til it is. Obviously, life is one practical joke after another, giving us opportunities to expand and to contract. Opportunities to break and to decide, do I let this take me out, or do I use it as medicine to allow myself to heal? I've no idea who, if any of them, will be a part of my life again.

Amazingly, I'm okay with this. More than okay. I'm free, from the inside, out.

Free to choose, free to love, free to speak, or not, free to forgive, free to say, "The door is always open," and free to draw a line in the sand. No matter what. No matter who. And to say, "This far and no further."

Free to live simply, free to simply live.

I love you, Sean. My son. I will always love you. It's okay. You're okay.

Best of all, I'm okay.

You'll be 25 in a few days. Happy birthday. Make it count.

I don't think suffering is necessary. Suffering happens.
It's what we do with it that matters. Will we use it as an excuse
for not doing something we dream of doing? Or will we lean into it
as the compost that fuels our leap forward?

4/9/18

The long wait is over. I won my SSID appeal, which has been pending for almost three years while I've lived on next to nothing. I've been denied twice and finally, with a lawyer, have won. Now the money is beginning to trickle in.

I'm very happy to be preparing to clear out the debris of Phases One, Two, and Three of Corey of the Jungle at Hale Ōhana Honua. I'm not sure if the jungle became a reflection of what was going on inside of me, or if what happened inside of me was a reflection of the jungle I was living in. Either way, the reflections no longer match. Too much has happened. Too much has been cleared inside of me. I'm ready for my jungle to reflect this.

I'm working with a contractor as we prepare to excavate the front 120x50 of my acre, for a permanent driveway. We're going to lay base course and gravel for the driveway and make the 16x16 platform into a 10x20 with a real bathroom. No more ship's port-o-potty, no more jungle bucket.

This is to be my staging area. I'm pushing further toward the back where I plan on building a home. Not a big house, but a solid one. On stilts for an ocean view.

It's a two-year plan. And it feels like a metaphor for the years I've already lived here, getting to know the contours of my jungle, excavating my insides, clearing the canopy, getting rid of the bugs, wallowing through the muck. Allowing in the light.

We cleared the land, literally uprooted the stumps. Opened the canopy to let in the light. Created the space for new structures, and new dreams and ideas. Then it got muddy. Weeds grew. The vines tangled and trees fell. My renaissance village fell into disarray. Because there were still things inside of me in disarray. And now there is clarity. It's time for the land to reflect that back to me.

Beneath everything we say is true is an agreement which is what makes it true.
If we don't agree, then we believe it isn't true.
By this logic, everything, and nothing is true.

SECTION TWO: LAVA

CHAPTER 16:
Evacuation

5/2/18

Earthquake alerts are moving down the mountain to the east. Centered in Pahoa area. It's terrifyingly bad at times. Sometimes it's just a little bit of a rocking motion. Then other times it feels like a big jerk, followed by rumbles, and shimmies. Just had another as I typed this - averaging 10 an hour.

My neighbor and I drove up the block to check out the cracks in the road, on Pohoiki Road and Kahukai in Leilani Estates. We slept with our cars pointed out, just in case, with the earth beneath us jerking and rumbling as lava pushes its way through tunnels a tenth of a mile below.

It's calmed down which hopefully means it's just flowing smoothly beneath us and will find its way to the sea without erupting on land.

5/3/18

My foot next to the cracks. By the following day these widened and 'became the first eruptions in Leilani Estates.

I was at the pond today.

This morning, on my way home from a doctor's appointment in Pahoa, there was a big pink cloud eruption at Halema'uma'u, Pu'u'o'o, the caldera that's part of Kilauea.

Why did I go to the pond when there are earthquakes and cracks in the ground? I went because it's what I do, and because it was hot, and because I've never been in a situation like this. What was I was supposed to be doing? No one else was panicking, so why should I?

I wasn't here for the eruption in 2014, which threatened to cut Puna District off from the rest of the Big Island. In the back of my head, I think I've always thought that that near miss ensured my safety now. Like lightning never striking the same place twice, neither would lava flow where it had just recently been. Except the lightning thing is a myth.

I was here for the flow last year on the western flank. Even though it was within 20 miles of me, and people would often ask me if I was afraid to live so close to an active volcano, I wasn't. It didn't feel like a threat. Partly because it felt unreal, with droves of tourists hiking out to see it. I mean, how dangerous can something be if you can walk right up to it or ride a bike out toward it for a picnic.

Floating in the pond today felt different. There was an electric buzzing beneath the surface of our beautiful afternoon. The swarms of earthquakes (most of them higher than 3.0 and coming every three to four minutes) were acting as a deterrent to tourists. My friend Mango was there, so we hung out talking about what might happen, and there were others whose names I don't know who joined in, which is what happens at the pond. That's part of its charm. So, they talked, and I listened, and I was happy to invest in whichever theory kept me and my home safest.

I wasn't thinking when I left that this might be the last time I'd ever be here or see my friend.

Normally I stay at the pond until close to dusk, getting out in time to take a beach shower before the sun goes down. Today I decided to leave early, around 4:30 p.m. There isn't very good cell service there, so I didn't know anything was up. I headed for Pohoiki Beach Park for the sunset. I was thinking I might camp for the night instead of going home. I had Lily with me, and my minivan is always ready for an adventure. It was another perfect day in paradise at my favorite camping spot, watching the surfers, and the honu (sea turtles) along the shore.

When I got to Pohoiki, which is a mile up the road, something felt not quite right. Askew. I was agitated. I turned off my engine and turned it immediately back on. I felt an urgency. I wanted to go home. And I still had no cell service.

I don't usually drive fast. The windy drive up Pohoiki Road, through old growth mango trees, coconut groves, and sweeping vistas of Mauna Loa, are too beautiful to let fly by. In most places it's a one lane only "Puna pave," meaning it's uneven, no lines, and no shoulders, weaving its way around the big trees, sunlight flickering through the branch's high overhead. Today I didn't feel leisurely. I had no eyes for scenery. I drove fast, not knowing why but I found out soon enough.

One after another, I saw dozens of emergency vehicles, their lights flashing, coming in and out of driveways. And then, finally within cell range, my phone started to blow up. There were messages from Civil Defense, and from friends checking to see if I was okay. A fissure had opened up in Leilani Estates, and mandatory evacuations were in place there, and for us in Lanipuna Gardens.

By the time I got to Hinalo Street, my street, it was deserted. It felt abandoned. I felt alone like I never feel in my jungle. My neighbors were already gone or were hunkered down inside, which I was considering doing too, in the hope of evading the evacuations.

I ignored the Civil Defense alerts and drove down my street. It felt surreal. Blurry. I was watching my breathing, as if by controlling it, I had control over everything else. How had this happened so fast, when just last night I was outside my wagon watching a dozen wild pigs run down the street. That should have been a clue right there.

My land and wagon, my home, are at the end of a dead-end road, and my neighbors were there waiting for me. They'd come to check on me, to make sure I had somewhere to go. They said that they were leaving.

So, I turned around. I'd made my decision. I was leaving too. It felt scary. Dramatic. Surreal. If I stayed, I knew those feelings were going to get worse. I felt out of control. There were helicopters buzzing overhead, and smoke from fissure 1 was billowing across the rise. My eyes felt too big in their sockets. My brain was racing, processing in large print...not many words on a very large piece of paper.

I didn't stop to grab anything. I'll come back tomorrow. I thought. It's going to go to the ocean, and it's like they said at the pond, this will ebb and flow and we've got plenty of time before anything big really happens. I had no reference point.

I didn't know where I was going. Without thinking I called my friend Eric.

I think I said, "Hey."

"I wondered when you'd call, come on over," was his response.

I don't remember the drive to his place, except for the part where I passed his driveway in Nanawale Estates twice before I saw it and turned in.

Now I sit, my eyes doing this thing, this searching thing, like my mind is trying to find the edges of this strange new world, searching for the words that must be held on reserve for moments like this, when your normal everyday words are inadequate to the task. When you're trying to make sense of something that only happens to other people. Or people in movies, in some distant place, on some other planet.

What's next? I wonder. I don't have a "this is what to do when lava flows" checklist.

I'm also excited. This qualifies as an adventure. I'm at ground zero, witnessing a volcanic eruption, and it doesn't feel real. It doesn't feel like it's going to last long. No need to get dramatic or freaked out. Pele brought me here, she won't take my home away from me. She won't take my things. Not when I've finally worked out a plan. Not after all I have learned.

Eric is talking and I'm hearing every other word. Thoughts are pushing each other out of the way for my attention.

Then one wins.

"I'm going to lose my place." I said.

"Yes." He replied.

> *It bugs me when humans say Pele is pissed.*
> *Pele is just doing what she does, creating more planet,*
> *clearing paths, paving new ways with passion and intensity.*

5/3/18

Live feed
https://www.youtube.com/watch?v=FnPEv80AZo0&feature=youtu.be

...That's where it's erupting. There's my home...

5/6/18

> *This morning I awoke from a dream of bodysurfing in a river of lava.*
> *The lava was flowing freely, overtaking people, burning buildings and trees,*
> *and I thought it would burn me too. Instead it picked me up, carrying me along.*
> *Guess this is what I get for living at the bottom of volcanic slopes. (8/15/15)*

The Day I Got In

The sound of adrenaline. That's my voice. I hate hearing it. I want to be calm; I want to be collected. I can feel it below the surface of my skin, and I know it's what keeping me going, but I'm concerned it might be clouding my judgment. Or that it's making me into some kind of drama queen.

And at some point, giving myself permission to navigate this thing as best as I can, suspending judgment as to whether I'm doing it 'right,' or whether someone watching is going to call me out on how I'm responding. Like it's anyone's freaking business how I respond to a volcanic eruption. Like I don't have the right to be worried about my stuff. Like I am supposed to be okay and act normal. I admit, I've no idea the proper etiquette for an eruption.

I've been trying to get into my place all day. Eric was with me for a couple of hours as we drove up and down the highway to Kapoho and down Red Road, trying to get in. They announced this morning we could go in, but I keep getting turned away by Civil Defense.

When I did finally get in, Eric had gone home but I wasn't going to miss my window so went in alone.

Again, that eerie feeling, just like the day we were evacuated, of driving up my street, that disturbing emptiness. And I had to pee.

Just as I go to cop a squat, a truck pulls up. And it dawns on me how very alone I am in here. This person doesn't belong here, he isn't my neighbor, even though when he pulled up, he said he was. So, I did what we do on my street when strangers drive by, I held up my phone to take his picture, and I messaged my friends to tell the sheriff.

And I turned back to my land.

My breathing was raspy from the smoke in the air and there was a grape Kool-Aid smell which could have been burning fruit trees, or maybe chemicals from the nearby Puna Geothermal Venture (PGV). So many helicopters were overhead, I was that close to six open fissures. I stood there looking at my dying trees, their leaves inches thick upon the ground, covering the tin roofing that made my path. Thank goodness for that tin roofing, because it gave me a way to slide boxes out to my van. I'd never have been able to carry them.

I knew what I wanted to grab. I wanted my pictures. I knew where they were. I ripped (literally) open the storage tent on the platform because I knew they were in there. And I was hit by the crescendo of all the things I suddenly knew I wasn't going to be able to save. How to decide what to grab when I can't grab it all. I'm alone, and then again, this might be over in a day. Do I risk climbing up on the platform, and getting to the back where the pictures are, when I'm in here all alone? What if I fall or get hurt? Aren't I being ridiculous?

So, I grabbed. I looked around. I looked down into my crater, and up into my trees, my eyes trying to memorize, as they always did, the look and the lay and the way of my land. I looked at the wagon, and the stumps of the trees we'd cut down to make room for me to live, and I thought of where my decorations were, buried behind a stack of pallets I'd thought were cleverly protecting my things from rippers. But now they were beyond where I could reach, the vines and weeds entwined with them, holding them in place. I had no way to save what mattered to me most.

And wouldn't we just be coming home soon anyway, I thought for the umpteenth time.

Getting any of the boxes to my van was hell. I used to be strong, but now I'm not. I've had fatigue and chronic pain for too long. I'm weak. I hollered, because I could, as I got them to my van in any way that I was able, pushing, dragging, and shoving, knowing I'd pay for this tomorrow, and not willing to care about that until then.

Then I went inside my wagon. What to take? I turned in circles, my eyes darting. I started tossing important papers I didn't realize I'd forgotten into a plastic trash bag. I grabbed whatever I could. Clothes, medications, I looked at my silk blanket and decided, nah, it'll be here, and it needs to be washed. It's strange the things we think in such moments.

I emptied out my desk drawers. Pens. Lip gloss. I don't know, I don't remember. I was breathing hard, I was in so much bloody pain, my back was screaming, and I was scared. I was dripping with sweat and my throat hurt. It felt futile to grab these few things and to leave so much behind. I remember wanting my on-demand, hot water heater but couldn't hold my attention long enough to find a screwdriver to take it down.

In the end, I got out that trash bag, and seven boxes. I glanced in a few of the boxes but didn't want to take a longer look. If I don't look, I won't know for sure what's gone.

As I drove away, I said goodbye again. Goodbye number two.

> *Beautiful clear night, (except for the vog), lots of food, kids playing,*
> *animals running around. Hawaiian music drifting through the air...*
> *lava flowing a few miles away. If it weren't for that you'd think this was a party.*
> *(5/5/18 at evacuation center)*

5/6/18a

Live feed
https://www.youtube.com/watch?v=MZ9FiWsMcto&feature=youtu.be

...we're trying to get into my property, Civil Defense said the evacuation is lifted to retrieve important papers, but the National Guard is not allowing me to go in...

...there are fissures about and below Leilani Avenue, so we're going to wait...

CHAPTER 17:
Going In

5/7/18

Live feed
https://www.youtube.com/watch?v=HIj7ybOj750&feature=youtu.be

...there are reports of Civil Defense allowing people in, but the alerts say the emissions are too high, so the barricades are up...one minute roads are open, the next they're closed...
...it's possible I won't lose my land...my things will be there, and the wagon will be there...
...watching this may be uncomfortable but it's real...
...why would anyone live on the side of a volcano?
...30 homes have been lost and I'm not sure how many structures. In Puna, "structures" usually means a house without a permit. I think we're up to 12 open fissures...
...staying at the evacuation center is easier than being in someone else's home, for me and for Lily...

5/14/18

Maybe I should have waited a little longer before taking my free helicopter ride. I was so sure that the eruptions were going to end though and didn't want to miss the opportunity to see it from above. It ended up being the last time I'd see my home, and because I'd chosen a helicopter without doors, and it was terrifying, I wasn't able to hold on for dear life (like that would save me if we suddenly plummeted to earth) and take pictures at the same time.

Seeing the line of the fissures cutting through Leilani looked beautiful and strange. It was obvious that the eruptions were following a straight path and heading out of Leilani toward the ocean. So even though my land was dead and brown, the only color being the tarps and structures left behind, the lava seemed far enough away, and going even further.

This is a piece of tephra that landed on Ikaika Marzo's foot while he was out doing updates for the evening hub live feeds. Aila'au is The Forest Eater and enemy to Pele.

That was before the energy shifted from the graceful beauty of Pele, to the rampaging outrage of Aila'au, The Forest Eater. If we needed further indication of his presence, it was provided the day this piece of tephra landed on Ikaika's foot.

The final questions I posed in my email to Paradise Helicopters (below) remain largely unanswered, and there aren't likely to be any answers now that the land is covered in lava.

Not until the eruptions were over did we find out that the explosions we heard at night at the evacuation center were coming from Lanipuna Gardens, and caused by an explosive lava the geologists didn't know existed in the Lower East Rift Zone (LERZ). This left behind a crust of lava called shelly pahoehoe, which looks solid, but isn't, and collapses inches, or many feet, beneath the slightest weight.

I'm grateful for the last glimpse I got from the helicopter before the rest of everything happened.

On Sunday, May 12, after messaging Paradise Helicopters about a flyover of my place, I received their response. I was asked for proof of residence and something indicating I had been evacuated from my home. Upon their receiving this information I was offered a complimentary seat for the following day. Below is my thank you letter to them. As you can see I also asked the questions they had no answers for. My brain was searching for answers wherever they might be found.

May 13, 2018, 11:21 PM
To Paradise Helicopters

Thank you so much for the opportunity you so generously provided me with this morning.

Our pilot was able to fly directly over my place, allowing me to see with my own eyes what's happening. I was evacuated the first day. Since then I've seen aerial pictures that were confusing, distant, and blurry.

Although there's nothing I can do, and Lanipuna Gardens remains off limits, it gave me some relief to at least see it's still there.

I wish I'd been able to take a picture to really study what's going on. The surrounding homes are still green, but my place is straight up brown. The trees are skeletons. It was very lush and wild jungle.

I'm wondering, is it possible that sulfur emissions are what's killing my land faster than the areas around me? I have a 50-foot crater, and a 200-foot rift that leads to a steam vent cave and ends in an eruption cone beneath the earth. Is it possible these are emitting sulfur dioxide but not steaming? Is this something CD or HVO should know about? The difference between my place and the surrounding ones was just clear.

Thank you again.

Be well, be wild,

Corey

5/15/18

Live feed
https://www.youtube.com/watch?v=w5xS31UDBCo&feature=youtu.be

...*Halema'uma'u, which was overflowing with lava on May 1st, is empty now...and is like looking into the mouth of a monster...especially terrifying in a leaning helicopter without doors...*
...*Today the crater started erupting ash up about 12,000 feet into the air...*
...*Our air has been fairly clear today. We do have N95 masks but still no carburetors available for the respirator masks...*
...*The erupting fissure count is at 19...Pohoiki Road is cut off. There's no way in anymore. My home is still there.*
...*Reports are circulating that it could be up to five years before we can return home...*
...*I'm told that it's easier on me because I didn't have a real house...I don't think this is easier on anyone...whether families with kids, elderly, or in your twenties...I'm single, so I don't have to take care of anyone else...but I'm single, so there's also no one to help me...*
...*Fissure 6 is active again, that's very close to my home...*
...*Facebook fills a void that the county isn't even trying to fill...*

CHAPTER 18:
Parking Lot Life

5/29/18

Evacuees in the parking lot. Without the help of each other, the Pacific Baptist Church, Pu'uhonua o' Puna (the Hub), and many other churches and individuals helping, we would be in even more dire straits. Red Cross has done nothing. When I ask them a question about something going on out here in the parking lot, they tell me they have nothing to do with us, that the parks are in charge out here.

So, because Red Cross is not in charge, they don't help? No one else is pouting or worrying about who's in charge. They are just doing all they can to help.

Meanwhile, when Red Cross isn't busy sulking, they occupy themselves with putting up yellow caution tape to keep people in rows, and when donations come in, they are scooted through the gym into the back storage. They say they do this to stop people from hoarding. Hmm. Who's doing the hoarding?

They have dozens of new cots in boxes, not being used. When a new person moves into the parking lot and asks to use one, unless they ask the right person, they are denied. I got one because someone snuck it out for me. The same goes for anyone needing a tent, which they also have stacks of.

Sitting on the supply table, which at first was overflowing with canned goods, toiletries, and new socks and underwear, are five cans of peas, one jar of BBQ sauce (we aren't allowed to BBQ in the parking lot), baby food, diapers, and tampons. Sometimes cookies. Those same items, in those exact amounts have been there for a week. And you say you need water? You can have one for yourself, and one for your pet, per day. Who knows, there may be an emergency that necessitates having those 25 cases sitting on the gymnasium floor available at a moment's notice. Oh, wait. This is an emergency.

If you have a question, you can stand waiting for five minutes for one of the 10 people behind the yellow caution tape to acknowledge you. They look around you, or through you, or next to you, anything to not make eye contact. They spend a lot of time staring at each other, and at their computer screens.

Then suddenly, yesterday, two surly cops show up, walking the parking lot, asking unnecessary and intrusive questions. As if we are criminals who collectively conspired to lose our homes so we can live in a parking lot and get some free BBQ sauce.

It'll be fun, we said. Like a free ride.

Wake up, powers that be! We are NOT at fault here. We are NOT criminals. Do NOT treat us as interlopers when we are homeowners.

In two days it will be one month. What's the plan?

Crickets

> *Today was also the first day last year that the flow map said my place was gone. The next day the map said my place was still there. This continued for the next four days 'til I went to Ikaika, who contacted Bruce who was able to send me a photo from the helicopter that it was gone. (5/27/19)*

5/30/18

Rippers and Tweakers

I recently wrote that those of us living in the parking lot aren't criminals. But some are.

I know that drugs don't make a person, and that people aren't in their right minds when they're on them. That's where I draw the line though when it comes to what they're responsible for.

One morning, just a few days after I got here, a small tent popped up by the light pole across from me. Why she chose this spot I'm not sure because it's also where the rubbish can is. She admitted that she isn't an evacuee, she was just tired of paying rent and decided to move into the parking lot.

A few weeks into the eruptions, other unfamiliar faces began to show up. Some official told Red Cross to not turn anyone away, so the homeless from Kona were hopping on the bus to ride across Saddle Road to come live amongst us. And why not, free hot meals, and a tent. Woohoo!

There were also the rippers and the tweakers, who were there almost from the start.

Tweakers and rippers are kind of the same thing. They rip so they can tweak. And in the parking lot we have our share. They prefer the dugouts, where they put up tarps so no one can see in. Some even put padlocks on the gate, which we aren't allowed to do. According to the Park's guys they have to have access to everything.

Somehow these guys get away with it and are creating little compounds in there with tarps for screens and multiple tents, with people coming and going all day. Any attempt to stop this has been futile because they are on foot. In order to come in by car you need a placard and ID, but no one can stop anyone from walking in through the bushes.

Then there is the woman who was caught in the middle of the night with a wheelbarrow, stealing from the donations tent and hoarding what she took in her dugout. This is the same woman who first lived in the small tent by the light pole. But who'd moved into a dugout when someone else moved out. Totally bizarre because everything she took, she could have walked in during the day and taken for free.

I went out one day, a day or two after the eruptions began, and came back to see a group of people had moved in next to me, and of all things, as I walked up, the guys started trying to pick up on me. I don't know if you've watched my videos but caring about makeup and hair is the last thing on my mind. Not only was their behavior offensive, it was disturbing. They were obviously drunk, and their spinning eyes were a dead giveaway that ICE (meth) was involved. I didn't feel safe, I knew my things weren't going to be safe, and my head was too full of everything else to try and figure out what to do.

So I played nice while my friend went to security who told me to take off for a while. When I got back, they had moved the waste-oids out to the ball park AND put up a blockade of orange cones next to me so now no one can move in behind them. The Park's guys ROCK.

I did find out later that they, or someone, had stolen the entire arm of my windshield wiper off the minivan. Not just the blade. The arm.

There were hundreds of us living in the parking lot at any given time, helping each other put up tents, move pallets, or serve food. But this handful of people made it impossible for us to continue to feel safe. Their presence emphasized how much we had lost, how precarious our lives now were, and how long we'd been living in a parking lot.

Donators vs. Donatees

It shouldn't be an Us and Them game. No one gets out of this life alive, and no one gets out of it unscathed. At some point, you will be the one in need. Important to think about before altruism clouds your judgment.

A man gave me a pat me on the cheek today. Said, "See, that's a good job sweetie, I knew you could do it."

He. Patted. Me. On. The. Cheek. WTF.

He has no idea how close I came to patting him by the balls. I swear, if the rage could have flown out the roof of my head it would have burnt us all on its way back down. But I held my personal eruption back.

I had walked up from my van to the community center where a group was donating pillows and toiletries, and hand sanitizer (which we go through by the gallons). They had other things like toothpaste and brushes, which I declined. I have enough of those for the next five years. And tampons and pads. If I still needed those, damn, I could have saved myself thousands of dollars for years to come. But I don't. I just took what I needed. A pillow, sanitizer, and a washcloth.

At the end of the line you sign your name and give them your former address. And show them your arm band. Which I'd forgotten. Shite.

There I am, over a month into this thing, in a tank top and pareo, leaning on my cane with one hand while holding the pillow in the other, and obviously struggling. And the man says, "No, no, we can't let you go without the wristband." I point up the parking lot to my van. I point at Lily who's outside waiting for me. I point at my cane. I point out my labored breathing. I say, this is a long walk for me. "No, no, sweetie, I believe you but you're going to have to go get it."

I stick my head inside the door to the Red Cross volunteer table. The woman sitting there has seen me now for weeks. We exchange hellos every time I walk through the door. She's met my cat. I say, "Hey, I forgot my arm band, can I have another?"

"I'll need your identification for that."

WTF. Just then Donovan, one of the volunteers who's from here and has been at the evacuation center since the first day, walks up. "Can you vouch for me?"

He looks at the volunteer. "You know her."

"Yes but..."

"You know her. Give her a new fucking band."

Which is when I walked back outside where the guy patted me on the cheek and called me sweetie and said, "See, I knew you could do it."

I'm going to generalize here, so bear with me, there are always exceptions to the rules. But why.

Why is that when people help people, they tend to patronize them? As if whatever disaster they've just been through has turned them into children who don't know better? Is it motivated by sympathy? Is it born of low self-esteem? Is it grown from the misplaced concept that disasters make us dumb? Or that we are to blame for being in the wrong place at the wrong time, and therefore someone else now knows what's best for us?

Yes. And no. Some people are just that way.

But this guy was judging me, and it showed. My tank top and pareo and my messy hair and my cane, they all painted a picture that he made an assumption about. Instead of assuming I am a homeowner, that I hold multiple degrees, not to mention my black belt in mouth karate, he took one look and assumed it would be okay to call me sweetie, and to pat me on the cheek. Condescending old man.

And this is what it's been like for most of my time in Puna, not just now during the evacuations. Being underestimated. Questioned. Here it's just accentuated. There's the them, who rushed across an ocean to save us, and there's us, who don't need saving, we just need a pillow and some sanitizer. We didn't lose our brains because we lost our land. You aren't better than us because you chose not to live on lava.

And my assumption is that all of this is true. That it's not just me being ultra-sensitive because I hate asking for help. Or me resenting that because I've been sick, no one knows that once upon a time I was formidable. That back in the day, no man, or woman would risk patting me on the cheek and calling me sweetie, as if I was a three-year-old.

Aaaah. It's all true. The assumptions, the patronizing patting, and the codification of the idea that people in crisis need your sympathy, when what they really need is your empathy and the helping hand of a peer, not a parent.

This is how dependency is created. You're not special because you're helping. You're an angel for helping, and that's where it ends. Because tomorrow it could be you needing the help, and how you gonna feel when the woman you helped yesterday talks to you like a child today? Nothing has changed but the chair where you sit.

Let's give the survivors of trauma the respect and recognition they deserve. Let's assume they are capable instead of broken. They are the ones who are gaining wisdom from the experience. That's a terrible gift. Don't make it worse by patting them on the cheek.

CHAPTER 19:
Red Cross

5/8/18

Where are my Red Cross friends?

Mr. C, the 'head guy' here, needs a take down. I was given a futon to replace my wet mattress in the van. I saw it was wet and torn, and laughing, said, "I've already got one like this" and asked for one that wasn't. He said, as he was walking away, "We'll give it to someone who isn't a complainer and actually appreciates our help."

Mr. C is the FIRST and ONLY person, to-date, who's been anything but helpful and supportive. When another volunteer, who is also an evacuee, saw what Mr. C said to me and called him on it, that person was told to "stand down."

WTF. Mr. C, you have no idea who you've just messed with.

When it was taken to HIS supervisor, that person excused his behavior, and dismissed it, saying that Mr. C "is stressed and tired." Are. You. Kidding. Me. Mr. C is maybe in his thirties, only just arrived, and most decidedly NOT losing his home to lava. Yet we are supposed to make accommodations for him. Hmm.

If Mr. C is stressed after one day, he's in the wrong job.

Mr. C, I'm quite possibly about to become your worst nightmare.

Why am I making a big deal of this? Because it is. And if he's like this on day one, and his supervisor isn't going to hold him accountable, then he's only going to get worse.

Mr. C, you need to be held accountable.

Or, maybe not. It turns out that his Red Cross supervisor is also his mother. For real.

It's cold tonight so I'm wearing my hot knee socks. I'm quite the sexy beast.

5/20/18

Last night's community meeting with the Red Cross egomaniacal buffoons didn't go well. They are only saying what the real Big Wig buffoons, who aren't even here, have told them to say. People here are mostly good, and kind, just sorely misinformed.

From the beginning of the eruptions, and subsequent evacuations, we've had incredible support from our community. There has been a 'get it done' attitude by the local Red Cross volunteers who live here, and were immediately on the ground.

Then Red Cross personnel began arriving from the mainland.

They didn't take a lay of the land. They didn't spend any time observing what was here, who was here, and what was working. We live under a unique set of circumstances, unique even in Hawaii, even when a volcano isn't erupting.

Because of this, the Red Cross has created a clusterfuck. They have alienated those they are here to serve. They haven't bothered to try to get to know us, or to understand our community. They have created a secretive, hierarchical, ego-driven machine of 'us vs. them.'

Their most common response to a question is, "I'm new here, I don't know." There's no follow up of, let me see what I can find out. There is no sense of community and the attitude of 'just get it done' is missing. They are not here as allies.

They adhere to a patriarchal, paternalistic, and patronizing structure of 'we know what's best.' For those of us here, who are largely landowners and homeowners, we are used to a high level of independence and self-sufficiency. We are accustomed to our rugged terrain. We know best how to survive in our harsh environment of rain, wind, and now lava and fires. Yet, our input, which could be invaluable to these muggles, is being ignored in favor of the 'policies' of the overarching Red Cross bureaucracy.

People are not policies. We are not children. We are resilient, hardy pioneers living in an area that is often referred to as the Wild West of Hawaii.

From the beginning, it's made all the difference for us to have our animals with us, and to be able to maintain our privacy. Now we're being told that they're taking these things away. From nursing moms, and seniors, and everyone in between. Anyone who wants to be in a tent is being moved to spray painted squares in the grass. No ground tarps, no overhead tarps. Just mud.

They are issuing arm bands of different colors that disallow us entrance into the community center. I asked them if we would soon be receiving gold star patches to sew on our clothing, or our red letter 'A's.' They didn't get it.

The agency as a whole has been made immune to their dehumanizing policies and procedures. We don't need them. We don't want them. We didn't ask for them. As a community we were doing just fine. As I said, we are resourceful and resilient. They've brought nothing to the mix but confusion, disrespect, and now anger and resentment.

I am wondering why the Red Cross has been given so much power to do as they see fit, without consulting those they've supposedly come to help. I am curious about their monopoly in disasters and evacuations, when a simple Google search illustrates that what I'm describing is in no way unique, but rather the norm. Who sits on their board, who is profiting?

With proper training and orientation, the good people who volunteer could be doing good things. As it is, they are only serving to make a challenging situation more difficult.

Bottom line, they may not like how we choose to live, they may not understand how we do it. But it's our choice. We are evacuated, but we are not under martial law. The churches should not have to go to the extreme measures they are in order to smuggle ice, tarps, dry blankets, or fresh fruit into the evacuees in the parking lot.

I thought long and hard about whether or not to speak out. As individuals many of them have helped me a lot. But. This is a mess.

The Red Cross began as a non-governmental agency but has become the go-to corporation, in essence, for all disasters. They have a monolithic monopoly that magnetizes government funding, and lines the pockets of their revolving-door board membership.

It is hard to not give in to the apathy of 'knowing' that speaking up won't change a thing.

But if not me, who? And if not now, when?

*There were a handful of people who took offense to this when
I originally posted it on Facebook. But there were hundreds who shared it,
and thousands who commented, many of whom had their own or similar stories of
frustration and disappointment. Stories going back to WWII and up to the current day.
Yet, nothing changes. My question remains, if Red Cross is a non-profit organization, why
does it have a monopoly on crisis situations? I'm not an expert in how these things work,
but shouldn't there be some sort of healthy competition for the resources?*

CHAPTER 20:
The Situation

On Fri, May 25, 2018, 6:24 PM Corey <<u>corey@farhorizons.org</u>> wrote:

Re: Update

Aloha

My apologies for the long silence. I had no words.

As most of you know, I live in Hawaii.

What many of you don't know, is that I live in lava zone 1, in Lanipuna Gardens. I was among the first to be evacuated on May 3rd, after the first eruption.

I was not allowed into my home. I drove in and was redirected out of the area. I have been allowed to return once, on day 3, briefly, to retrieve important papers, and a few belongings. The ground was already thick with dying leaves caused by the never-ending flow of gas emissions blanketing our tiny subdivision.

While I was there the 7th eruption occurred, about a tenth of a mile from my home. I was ordered to get out NOW. It was eerie, and scary, and smelly, and sad.

The emissions have continued to billow across my home, and the homes of my friends and neighbors. Many of them have already lost their homes, and even more are being threatened.

On day 6, Paradise Helicopter Tours generously gave me a complimentary flyover in order to see what I could see.

At that time, my place was still there. From the air up above, my lush jungle looked to already be completely dead, turned brown from the hazardous levels of SO_2 it's been blanketed in. My acre of lush rainforest reduced to skeletons of trees.

My tiny home, my gypsy wagon, was still there, as was my awning and my platform. I could tell only because they were the only spots of color remaining on the landscape. My magical wagon survived a previous flow from Kilauea in the 80s, and I'm holding onto the Hawaiian belief that if a home survives once, it is protected from being threatened again.

The status of my place is currently unknown. Eruptions 1 through 17 have been running parallel, about one tenth of a mile from me, for almost 3 weeks. Eruption 20 was on my street, on the other side of Pohoiki Road, and headed toward me. It got to the stop sign, again, about a tenth of a mile away, and turned left. It joined eruptions up to 22 and those are the ones hitting the ocean now. There is also lava pooling, which is creating lava lakes that are spreading across homes and farmlands below me. Earlier eruptions that had stalled are flowing again at the bottom of my street.

There is no way in anymore. No more flyovers are allowed due to the danger of the fountaining eruptions, and to the extreme toxicity of the air.

This morning we awoke to another concern, one our community has been fighting for many years. The flow is moving closer to the geothermal plant (PGV), which practices fracking in the lava tubes of the Lower East Rift Zone. Which is exactly where all the eruptions are. Coincidence? Doesn't matter anymore. It's maybe, maybe, two tenths of a mile from my home.

The lava has breached the perimeter and is heading for the wells. PGV says they've been quenched, and capped, with thick steel. They have no idea if it will make any difference. If/when the flow hits those trapped gasses, even the scientists don't know how bad it could be. My home may survive the lava, only to be swallowed up in an explosive, toxic, man-made, idiotic abyss.

I am currently staying at the Red Cross evacuation center. My being here allows me to stay as informed as possible, and to access resources in order to plan for the future.

Even if the flow was to stop right now, and the lava to not hit PGV, it will take many months to cool, many more months, or years, to clear the roads, and more time on top of that to make the land habitable again.

There is no insurance for lava zone one, except in isolated instances. I paid cash for my land, my entire savings. None of us knows how long this is going to last, or if our homes will survive. Even if the eruptions stop today, it's going to be months, or even years before most of us can go home.

As for me personally, all but a few of my things were left behind. My home, my tools, my pictures, my Christmas ornaments, my heirlooms, my treasures, and memories, so here I am, hoping for the best, and planning for the worst.

And wanting you to know that I'm still planning to be at Far Horizons this summer but needing you to know that these extreme circumstances have kept me from being more available to you as we approach the season.

It's my honor and privilege to support you and your workshop attendees.

Be well, be wild.

Corey Hale
Far Horizons
Camp Director

CHAPTER 21:
The Mourning

5/31/18

I stopped to breathe and, on the exhale, began to cry. The kind you can't stop, the kind that feels like you're all heat, and endlessness, bottomless grief.

I chose to live on the side of a volcano, we all did. Others choose to live where there are fires, floods, hurricanes, or traffic accidents. That doesn't change the love we feel for our places. We accept the downside because we love the upside.

I don't think we have any more choice over the places we fall in love with than we do with the people who we love.

I've finally seen a picture that confirms that my home is gone. Totally gone.

This was taken moments after I left the Hub and Ikaika receiving the picture from Bruce that my land was covered in lava.

6/2/18

Live feed
https://www.youtube.com/watch?v=4chBJaQwDNM&feature=youtu.be

…I haven't made an update in a couple of days because it's really, it's really because of this [starting to cry], because it's been really hard to talk about it.

On Thursday I, um, I just couldn't, I just, I had been watching the flow maps and one day it would say my place was gone, and the next day it would say it was there. So I went down to the Hub, to Pu'uhonua o Puna, and Ikaika was there. I asked him if…[voice breaking] I tried to ask him, if he knew about my place and it just, it broke, it broke the damn on my fears and all of it.

I just started crying and got the same damn headache that I'm getting right now, and he sent a text to Bruce who had just come down from a helicopter and taking pictures. Ikaika gave him my address and in a few minutes, Bruce sent back a picture.

[crying]

This is why I haven't done a video because there's all this stuff, I should be doing better with this and not wanting to cry. So I looked at the picture and it took some time to orient myself because there aren't many landmarks left. And. I finally saw it..It's just, it's, um [voice faltering], it's a lava field, and it cut across my land. ...

...I try not to torture myself with it, but we've lost so much already. Our roads to anywhere in Puna are cut off...

...There are metal plates across the road to Kalapana, (because of the dozens of steam vents that have opened) and the lava river took out Four Corners today, Red Road is cut off at McKenzie Park. I'm not sure about the road to Kapoho. It's open to, I think, to people who live in there. But it's cut off Vacationland and Warm Ponds. Warm Ponds is still there, but there's no way to get there...

...It's just, when this is over, when we don't even know when it will be over. it's not a matter of, you know, digging through the rubble and finding what was there cause it's gone...

[long pause]

...I can't focus...

...It's not possible...

...It's not like this is, and I'm not saying that going through a fire, or a flood isn't awful, it's awful. There are differences. it's just not over. There's no, there's no, okay, it's time to clean up, and start again and the fissures that are above my land that are erupting. I mean, it's Leilani Estates is a, it's a pond. It's a lake of lava. And at any moment could just, you know, it's just the lava is just pouring all over the place now...

...A little part of me says all those treasures of mine [crying], you know, the, the things I've collected in my traveling, and my pictures, and the things I [crying], my Christmas decorations from when I was, you know, for my whole life. And just so many things that I don't even know. And I, I, I try to write them down and get them out of my head. Even my silly refrigerator magnets, you know, that I've been collecting for decades that were from every place I went are, you know, it's just, just all those little things that you pick up and reminds you of some good memories, some good thing that happened and who you were with...

...I can't even, I don't even understand for myself how much this hurts. Like it seems like it's just stuff. It's just, a lot of people have gone through so much worse and, but there's like a, like somebody like twisting my stomach in knots and there's just, there's just [crying], you know that feeling in your throat where you've just got to cry cause it hurts...

...I know that this will be okay, and I'll look back on it someday and be like, what an amazing experience. And I've had an amazing life and just really, my whole body hurts...

...I put everything, all of me into creating this and took this, you know, I took this big leap to move here and to buy land. You know, I've never owned anything. I've been a gypsy, I've never stayed in one place, and I fought really hard to stay

here and to, to bring my dream to life and you know, to hand clear my land…

…To not give up, and to know that because I owned my land free and clear because I had my gypsy wagon because I had, you know, had been collecting all the things that we're going to go into my house, you know, the marble countertops and the, wrought iron furniture, the, the just, just, just all the things that go into building your dream home…

…I knew because I paid for my land, I'd never had to pay rent again. That it was my place, I owned it. I always had a place to come home to, and that my stuff was safe, and, and it, nobody could take it from me…

…I feel sick…I have a terrible headache. I wake up almost every day to a headache, and to the ash in the air, and Pele's hair…right after I brush my teeth my mouth tastes like crap because there's just the ash…

…So many people have said you'll rise from this again. You always rise from the ashes. And it's true. You know, I've got major rise-from-the-ashes muscles, but I'm a little over it…

…I can't think…this is what most people are going through is we just can't think things through just this whole heart and gut and body and brain numbing…

…I finally moved back to Hawaii. I spent all my money on my land. I'm bringing this dream vision thing I've had forever to life. And then lava…

6/3/18

Live feed
https://www.youtube.com/watch?v=fBM7eHnhqJw&feature=youtu.be

…After turning off the video I was sick yesterday so called in a Red Cross nurse…what a fiasco of patronizing uselessness that was…

…Pastor Brian said if anyone is going to talk to you the way the Red Cross nurse did, they should at least bring popsicles… (he brought popsicles today)

…synchronicities that occurred before the eruptions…a new generator, a new hot spot…things were going so well that in my mind I was preparing for the best, not for this…

…the trees in the parking lot are dying from the vog…

…lava reached Four Corners in Kapoho and Green Lake went up in a cloud of steam…so Kapoho, Vacationland, the Warm Pond, and Pohoiki are cut off…no way in by land…

…I have canceled going to volunteer at Far Horizons…I just can't be so far away and out of touch…still planning on house-sitting for a month though…

…there's talk of a land swap…hell no…

…I want to go home…

CHAPTER 22:
I Want Out

6/8/18

Live feed
https://www.youtube.com/watch?v=rZHyy8C8OrY&feature=youtu.be

... (yelling, rain pounding in the background)

...Acid rain and seed clouds – causing insane rains just in Puna...I thought I'd try to show you what it's really like here...

...I'm over it guys. I'm over it. I want. Out...

...five-gallon buckets meant to hold down the awning are filling with Pele's Hair and it's what we're breathing when we don't have our masks on...

...this is crazy...every time it seems like it's slowing maybe a little bit and it feels like it's [the lava] almost over. It's not...

...disaster recovery groups are coming through offering help when this is over...but Puna has become a lava lake, what if it's just gone...then what...my plan was to have my home here, travel out there, then come back home for the rest of my life...now what, go pay rent?...

...I don't know what I'm feeling anymore...I feel like I'm me, and I feel like, what am I doing...

...I'm tired. One can only watch so much RuPaul's Drag Race. Well that's not true. I can watch it forever, but one can only watch so much RuPaul's Drag Race without getting your own drag on...guess I'll do that now...

CHAPTER 23:
Adapting

6/10/18

Our Routines

Each day brings more. It feels endless, waking up to the next terrible thing. Reaching for my iPhone before my eyes are open, looking for the next news on Facebook. Because that's where the most current information is. The information that people in our community are out there gathering for us. There are about a half dozen websites I check.

We all have our rituals. Most morning rituals sounded similar to my own. Evenings are different. My friend Imago watches Philip and John and Ikaika and their nightly updates from the Hub as she does the dishes before bed. I watch the videos from Bruce, and Mick, hoping for images of my place, trying to determine if it is there, or is it really gone?

Some people have been able to return to their homes. Some have done so out of necessity, to keep their belongings from walking away in the hands of rippers/looters. Legitimate residents, people like me, aren't able to get in, Civil Defense bars us from going home. But thieves? They keep finding a way.

And in the parking lot, the evacuation center, our encampment grows. Sturdy tents, and hefty awnings going up side-by-side-by-side, across multiple parking lots. We stretch from the parking lot I am in, into the dugouts in the ball field next to me, up onto the grass into the second parking lot across from me, and down below between the senior center, and community meeting rooms.

We don't know how long this is going to last. We are in limbo, and we are settling in for the long haul. This not normal setting, but we have begun to create our new normal.

In my set up, I began with just my minivan. But it got really muggy keeping the windows and doors shut in the rain so when someone offered me a 6x8 tarp, I hooked it over my open side door, and pinned it under my camp chair to keep it from blowing away. Then someone else offered me her clamshell tent which had collapsed in the heavy rains we are having. That went over the tarp, which offered more shelter from the endless rain.

My futon and blankets are still damp in the mornings, but it isn't terrible. The mold growing on the carpet in the front from lack of circulation, however, is.[7]

Why don't I have more tarps, or a tent, or an awning? Because as fast as any of the donation centers get them, they are gone. Rippers and tweakers, pretending to be evacuees, swoop in, take as many as they can, then go into Hilo and return them for cash. The centers have started marking the item tags with permanent markers, so the stores won't do returns, but that doesn't help us in the moment.

Going into Hilo isn't any better. We have a few big-box stores, Walmart, Target, and Home Depot. And their shelves are swept clean. I was able to get an expensive pop-up sun awning, and a draw-string tarp, something that's usually put on over the top of a sun awning. My parking lot neighbors have lent me one of their own tarps to use 'til I can get more of my own.

This meant I had a roof over my head (it leaked when it rained hard), and with my clamshell tent fabric and 6x8 tarp, I have been able to enclose two sides. Progress is slow but steady.

I continue to make rounds on my hunt for tarps. I go inside the community center to check at Red Cross, down to the Hub, into Hilo, and down to the Salvation Army truck. Mike, one of the security guards in the parking lot, just brought me a tarp, and Pastor Brian brought me two. They are all different sizes, most are 6x8, but I've got zip ties and am working magic with them. My windfall has been the tarp for a heavy duty 20x20 awning that was just donated, and my friend Rosi, who I met at the pond, one time, a few years ago, messaged Pastor Brian that she'd like to buy the poles ($300).

My home away from home is becoming cozy and more livable. I mostly stay dry. My tarps are now a multi-layered patchwork of green and blue tarps in different sizes and they keep out the worst of the winds. My 20x20 awning was put up over my 10x10 sun awning, leaving me a covered parking space for my van on one side, and room for pallets in the front, which is my lanai.

I forget I am living in a parking lot 'til I drop something and see the asphalt beneath my feet as I bend to pick it up. I've remedied that by putting down an outdoor carpet someone donated. I even put fairy lights up around my lanai.

---

[7] To see a photo essay of the evolution of the parking lot, visit www.coreyhale.com/gallery

6/10/18

Live feed
https://www.youtube.com/watch?v=at4VCwZXngE&feature=youtu.be

...Kazumi playing ukulele and singing her new song...Lily is around somewhere...

It's really true, if you build it, they will come. Our new normal. Sitting on my lanai in the parking lot, Kazumi playing ukulele and singing, Bobby and Imago coming to visit, the chicken man on his bike, bringing his chickens over so I can hold them because he knows I love them. We laugh, and cry, and wonder when it will end, and then we watch the sunset, and afterwards as the sky begins to glow red, as it does every night from the reflection of the lava against the night sky. Then the explosive booms, and the roar that sounds like a jet engine, the life of the lava takes over as the sounds of cars and people quiet down.

6/12/18

Live feed
https://www.youtube.com/watch?v=Ns_eOe8wrp0&feature=youtu.be

...today I'm hearing that it could be 10-15 years before we get back in...
...I've been concerned about leaving and missing whatever sort of support we're going to get...
...I don't want to let go of my land...I really don't...it's just...I want...maybe in six months I'll be ready to let it go...but right now [crying]...

CHAPTER 24:
Rough Time

6/13/18

Live feed
https://www.youtube.com/watch?v=sAV4HqRsoHU&feature=youtu.be

...I'm having a rough time and I'm having a rough time with having a rough time because I'm tired of having a rough time and I'm tired of saying I'm having a rough time, but I just, um, I just made the decision that I'm not ready to go to California right now. And my body kind of made that decision, because I guess as long as I am holding still, you know, staying in one place, whether it's in the evacuation center or whatever, it's still one place and it's stable and I know the people around me and I'm not alone.

As soon as I called to get my plane ticket, I just kind of melted down and realized I just can't leave here. I don't know, I don't know if that's right or wrong or sick, or...I have no idea how I'm supposed to feel [crying]...

I'm just following the clues that my that my body and my heart are giving me that say stay or go come, come or go, go, whatever, whatever, whatever, whatever. I, I don't, I don't see other people around me melting down the way that I am.

It's been six weeks today. It's been six weeks today since the first two cracks appeared. It'll be six weeks tomorrow since the eruption started. I have to stay here. I just feel. It's ridiculous. It's a beautiful home in Santa Rosa for me to house-sit in and, wonderful friends, but...there's also a lot of unresolved stuff waiting for me. Maybe not in tangible, physical form, but there's still a lot of stuff with people I'm related to back there that are a lot of loose ends. I'm just not, I'm not in an emotionally capable place of dealing with it right now.

...So, I'm going to stay in my parking lot...

...I'll be okay, but I'm not going to be okay if I leave here yet. I'm not going to be okay. If I go someplace where there's other things. Waiting for my heart to deal with. My heart is full enough right now and I don't know how one is supposed to act in an eruption. I don't, you know, I don't know. It would be good to see friends but there would be too much alone time...too much time to think...here in the parking lot I've got my space but I'm not alone...

...I've come into your living room to cry again. I guess this is just part of it and I just can't stand the idea of leaving Lily...

6/15/18

The following are short videos of the day I went into Leilani with my friends Imago and Bobby. This is fissure 8.

6/15a –

Live feed
https://www.youtube.com/watch?v=2Ugmemzl9ac&feature=youtu.be

…I'm going to see if you can see how close we are…My house, well my land now, whatever, whatever you call it at this point, it's in that direction. Maybe, maybe a quarter mile, but it's under lava and there's no road in…

…Every day is just like another punch to the gut…

6/15b -

Live feed
https://www.youtube.com/watch?v=WvfK8yKv4t8&feature=youtu.be

…they put more boards over the cracks in the road…

6/15c –

Live feed
https://www.youtube.com/watch?v=b-V_4NrI_0s&feature=youtu.be

…can you hear the roar? Holy crap…

6/15d –

Live feed
https://www.youtube.com/watch?v=c3Mp0n-rQfc&feature=youtu.be

…at the bottom right of that smoke you can see the actual heat of the lava going up into those clouds…

6/15e –

Live feed
https://www.youtube.com/watch?v=z9kZPG85rio&feature=youtu.be

…I don't know if there's enough definition for you to see how fast it boils up

and if I zoom it gets blurry, but it's SO2, and deadly quiet…

6/15f –

Live feed
https://www.youtube.com/watch?v=b89zFvw-7OE&feature=youtu.be

…watching fissure 8 from the end of a street in Leilani…holy shit… (Bobby)

6/18/18

Live feed
https://www.youtube.com/watch?v=MLGp8oG9Gl8&feature=youtu.be

…I was interviewed today for Smithsonian TV…I don't know when that's going to be aired. It may all end up on the cutting room floor. But they filmed Lily too so it would be cool if she got her 15 minutes of fame…

…I haven't been ready to talk to people on the phone who aren't here. Without meaning to, there's always that question of what are you going to do now? And it's not like it's over…

…people from all over the Big Island have been coming to offer massage in a Wellness Center [massage tables under an awning in the parking lot]. Now there's an offer for mental health and I'm going to be holding a coloring class…I used to offer Coloring and Conversation with Corey, at Kalani, and so now it's here…coloring is a great way to talk without putting anyone on the spot….it also occupies our monkey mind (anxiety) so the more important thoughts can be heard…

…there's been so much loss…and it's not only about how long you've been here, but how connected you were…what did it mean…

… what happened to questioning authority or, um, you know, or making YouTube videos, any kind of authority, and not thinking for yourself and jumping on the panic bandwagon. Like, holy cow. FEMA barges are coming to take us away… [more below]

…The sky is red, and the lava is flowing. I still want to go home…

CHAPTER 25:
FEMA

Newsflash:

CD Msg Aug 7 at 7:30AM. Eruption activity deceased. Fire Dept working Waikoloa, Kaalualu, and Keauhou Ranch fires. No threat to communities. No road closures.

Civil Defense alert where they once again dropped the ball.

It's as we feared. Civil Defense has mated with FOX News and given birth to an alternative universe where there's an eruption in Oahu on the Big Island, Kilauea has deceased, and you need to beware of flying lava fridges. (I actually caught a real one at the Hub).

News of flying refrigerators strikes fear in the hearts of evacuees. Not.

On another note, concerned citizens are warning evacuees of the approaching FEMA barges, known to be responsible for mass kidnappings. If you do catch sight of one of the FEMA barges (outside of the one video on YouTube), proceed with caution, extreme caution. Rumor has it they're hovering off the coastline and waiting to round us up. Just like they (allegedly) did with the Katrina refugees. Rounded them up and took them to concentration camps, never to be seen or heard from again.

People were panicking, packing their things and throwing their bags into their cars to get away from the evacuation center, which was ostensibly where the barges were headed. From a video. One video. In reality, FEMA has yet to arrive to assess the situation, much less round us up and take us away.

But the panic was real.

In response, I did what I do. Research. And what I found was zero. Zilch. Not even another YouTube video. Just the one.

Critical thinking could have saved us all a lot of adrenaline, which none of us needs more of. My words of advice are to consider caring as much about what you're feeding your brain as you do about what you feed your body.

You are what you watch. So watch carefully as you approach the planet's edge. We'd hate for you to fall off.

6/19/18

Live feed
https://www.youtube.com/watch?v=M6JaGS978Fg&feature=youtu.be

...I'm so bloody, freaking tired...

...I went to FEMA today, it was FEMA day and that meant driving to Keaau, which is like 10 miles from here or so. FEMA is set up at the high school in Keaau...

...You go in and you play musical chairs until you meet with a representative. Then they escort you to all the people who are there to help you. There are people to help with taxes. There's SBA [Small Business Association], and there's the USDA for agriculture...

...I signed up online because I received an email that said you should do so in order to start your case and to save time. Apparently, there's some mess-up in their computer system and they couldn't access my account, nor can I. They couldn't delete it either, which meant that they couldn't actually do anything FEMA-wise...

...Then I met with the Red Cross. The Red Cross can help with gas cards and gift cards, and I don't know what else, but they said it's enough to help...I tried to meet with SBA, but they've got a cockeyed system so after waiting an hour I gave up. I'll have to go back because you must be denied by SBA first in order to qualify for FEMA...

...This was all very grey area stuff because I'm not in the system, or I'm in

the system, but can't access me in the system so I'm not going anywheres anyways. So [laughing] I sound like a hillbilly anywheres anyways...

...I'm tired guys...I was there for four hours and I met with as many people as I could even if I didn't think there was a reason to...

...I can't get anything through Red Cross yet. I can't get anything until FEMA can access my records, and I can't move forward with anything else until I get the letter of property destruction which the county tax office sends. So that's going to take three to five days. Then I go back to Keaau to FEMA, and hope that the system is now allowing us to access my information and to move forward...

...My body hurts so bad...I hobble around like a little old lady and, I'm not a little old lady...

...Auntie Willie passed away...I didn't say sooner because I didn't want her family on Oahu to find out this way...So this really wonderful spirit has passed, who I never would've met if we hadn't been here at the shelter at the same time...She liked calling me a fake haole, which is redundant, making me a non-haole [laughing]. Anyway, then she found out that I was Jewish and so I became her Jewaiian...she was dying of cancer and she knew it. She held on to graduate with her three degrees. Amazing woman...

...Even though lava is erupting and we're living in tents, life still goes on. And then it doesn't...

CHAPTER 26:
Parked

6/25/18

Live feed
https://www.youtube.com/watch?v=GugNGp6gCkc&feature=youtu.be

...replacing the Marilyn Monroe doll from my grandpa with a Moana doll from Auntie Willie...
    ...replacing the handmade blankets from friends with blankets donated...
    ...I made a little replica of my gypsy wagon with Play-Doh....
    ...I'm in pretty good spirits actually...there are still a lot of things that I haven't remembered that I've lost that I'll remember over time...
    ...I think eventually, most of the time I'll be okay...

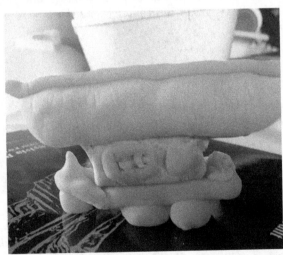

Recreation of my gypsy wagon out of Play-Doh...a little bit of art therapy.

    ...it's been eight weeks in this parking lot...all sorts of things go on...scandals...success stories...late night hookups...in tents...sigh...sound carries people...sound carries...
    ...Bad things can either bring out the worst or the best in us. And some people, like I didn't know April before this happened, but I've seen her since day

one. I've watched what she's created here. She hasn't done it alone, but she has been the hub and the motivation and the one willing to step up and take on all this responsibility. And when you take on that kind of responsibility, you don't always get thanked for it. People project all kinds of shit on you, such as you did it just so you could get all the best stuff, or you're being selfish. But you also get good recognition and gratitude, and tonight she was invited, or somebody suggested that she become a council person. She's got my vote because I've seen her handle her shit...

...I think that for so many people, this has created something they didn't have before...

...But I'm not having fun, you know, like it was to be living the way I was living, you know, in the wagon, traveling around in my van, getting a bit done here and there. But the last thing I did on my land I cut my leg to the bone on the tin roofing. I guess, thank goodness for injuries and delays or I'd have spent my money and that too would now be under lava...

...funny, but I'm not afraid. That's kind of surprising. I'm not afraid. You know, I went from having, owning, and not being in debt to, it's gone, and I've got nothing. And I'm not afraid...

...I haven't heard from my son. He's off doing whatever he's still doing. It's been almost a year and I guess he's got his own problems, his own situations to deal with. And. I'm surprised, you know, that...

...lava eruptions have a great way of putting things into perspective. They really do. And if he needs to not be in my life in order to have a good life, um, okay...no comment...

6/26/18

Live feed
https://www.youtube.com/watch?v=YvcF0bhyO8Q&feature=youtu.be

...today. Rough day, boring day. I colored. My skin's crawling and I'm going crazy with the lack of decisions. I just want to go swimming...I'm so tired of being in this parking lot and that it's finally coming to an end...

...I also heard from the Red Cross ombudsman about my recent email to them. I wasn't super patient with her, as it wasn't recent it's been almost two months...she wanted to know if she could share my email with others and have someone call me...I said sure, as it's been shared over a thousand times on Facebook, go for it...please only have someone call me if they intend to do something, otherwise don't waste my time....

...I know I'm going to write about this and am thinking Pema Chodron style, in essays...

...it's supposed to rain hard tonight...the Parks guys just came through and are bringing me another tarp to try to keep the winds out of my living space...I *had to wash a lot of stuff today because a cat is running around spraying on tents, and plus things get muddy fast...I try to make it homey...so when I step out in the morning it's onto a little rug and not immediately pavement...*

...I'm a Wander Woman, a gypsy girl and I do best with the unknown better than I do with having a lot of structure...I know how to find the form in the chaos...like putting together puzzle pieces...

...time for RuPaul's Drag Race...I finished the seasons I had so started over again. I must have been a drag queen in a former life...

Living in Puna is like living in a time when dinosaurs are being born. Dragons too.

CHAPTER 27:
Bored

6/27/18

Live feed
https://www.youtube.com/watch?v=g1KbDhWwxUA&feature=youtu.be

...another rough day...tough, boring day. I colored...I'm so bored that I sorted my towels and blankets...they're big donation items...which we need because of the rain...

I love homemade blankets because they're full of mojo and love from whoever made them...mine are gone in the lava and these are donated...anyway...I organized them...

...holding still is driving me nuts. I can't go far because my stuff is here. When I say stuff, I mean tarps and generators and basic living stuff that has been donated. The stuff keeping me dry and off the ground. I can't just take off and go to Kona like I'm used to, like I could go and leave my land and leave my generator and my gypsy wagon. I can't do that here because of the rippers and the tweakers. My gypsy wagon at home was closed with a bungee cord and I could still leave it for weeks at a time to go to the mainland, or house-sit, or go to the pond all day, and nobody would touch a thing. I feel stuck...

...while I was coloring, I heard from my son's wife, someone I've never met. Someone trying to stir up drama between my son and I...so interesting how people have no clue what it is we're dealing with here and think I'm going to be totally into their drama...and concerned about last year's news...I'd rather go to the pond...

...I'm glad I decided to not go to California where I'd be stuck in the middle of all of this...I don't need crazy-ass shit right now, and this is crazy-ass shit...I'm living in a parking lot, it's pouring rain, lava is flowing, and it's calm and peaceful...no crazy-ass shit...just coffee and friends...

...and Crocs...mine all got eaten by lava, but I've accumulated four new pair already...

...I'm going out of my mind...my skin's crawling...crazy with lack of decisions and the ability to go swimming...I want to go swimming...

...I'm not the only one...eight weeks ago we still had our dreams...

6/28/18

Live feed
https://www.youtube.com/watch?v=JU0W_XTZ_AY&feature=youtu.be

...I just got a lei, and I'm really happy because hot tea neighbor just came by...remember him? He was building a beautiful bamboo house across from me and he had the massive hibiscus flowers, and in the mornings, he'd bring a cup of hot tea over and leave on my doorstep if I wasn't awake yet...It felt really good to see him. He's been in California almost since this started, and just came back this week to check things out. It was funny because he pulled up and I knew I knew this person, but where from? It's only been two months. But the context has changed...

It's been eight weeks today since the last time I was in Warm Ponds. And it's moving day eve. I'm moving out of the parking lot...

...I'm just so happy to have seen my neighbor and to hear him say, I'm not giving up my land. I want to go in and rebuild. We just want to go home...

...I could go live with a friend...I've had a lot of offers...but, and I know this sounds crazy, I feel like I'm maintaining my independence by staying with other evacuees...I think there are seven of us moving to someone's land on Maku'u in Hawaiian Paradise Park (HPP)...just until the temporary housing is put up by the Hawaii Academy of Arts and Science (HAAS) property that was donated...

...Air quality is supposed to be really bad today. It's supposed to be really bad the next few days. I have carburetors for my gas mask now, as well as N95's for the ash...oh, and there were red ants on the boxes I moved...sigh...that never ends...

The lava is still flowing. I'm hearing rumors that they might designate fissure 8 as an actual volcano. I don't know if that's possible...also rumors that the Parks are talking about buying our land...don't see where that money would come from...

...I'm going to watch some more RuPaul's Drag Race because I really do want to be a drag queen. I think. I think I'd make a pretty solid drag queen...if you can't love yourself, how the hell are you going to love somebody else? ...

CHAPTER 28:
Things People Say

6/29/18

You know that moment when you're living in a tent in a parking lot, while the land you owned free and clear is under lava?

That moment when a lava river is running a few miles away, and your ex from almost twenty years ago calls to say he can't figure out if you're handling this really well or if you're just running a good scam.

And you say, "Huh?"

And he says, "What did you lose, a couple of boxes of pictures?"

Then you say, "Lose my number."

You know that moment, right?

Yeah, me neither.

Or that moment when you receive a letter from that same ex with a note on the flap that says, "Herein lies the solution to your lava problem." When you open the envelope an ad falls out for a woodchipper.

Yeah, me neither.

But just in case, fuck you, you pretentious, narcissistic, wannabe poser.

I'm so under this man-boy's skin. He couldn't control me in the past, and he sure as hell doesn't stand a chance of it now.

I mean, that is, if this had actually happened.

Then there's that moment
when another ex sends you a text
to say he had bypass surgery,
but that your life is the depressing one.

8/4/18

We're told how to feel, and we try, but what's real is somewhere in between. Between how we should feel, how we do feel, and how we wish we felt.

Pain and loss are not a competition. As long as you're keeping score, you're inviting more.

I won't compete with your pain by comparing yours to mine. We hurt. That's enough. Navigating it a certain way because it's the way Oprah,

Eckhart Tolle, or your Great Aunt Hilda says that's how it's done, doesn't mean it's better, smarter, or more enlightened.

It's one thing to choose a spiritual path and while upon that path come to an understanding that attachment to people, places, and things aren't in your best interest.

It's quite another thing to inflict that spiritual belief upon yourself or someone else after experiencing loss without choice; because you once read about the idea in a book or heard it at a workshop. Or read it in a meme. Or have fallen under the spell of the myth of positivity. That is merely ego pretending to be something it isn't. Distancing yourself from what's happening out of a sense of superiority and authority means there's a high probability you're going to miss what the experience is trying to tell you.

Contrast is a necessary and important part of being human, of becoming more of who we are. It's because we resist change that contrast often has to become painful in order to get our attention. Contrast creates our turning points, the places where we must change, or suffer more. These are threshold moments in our lives; they are our rites of passage.

What I'm saying is, pain is necessary when it comes to making the big changes. Or at the very least, discomfort. Unfortunately, we've been told it isn't. As if an oyster could make a pearl without the abrasiveness of sand. Adapting to making change without the impetus of pain is something to aspire to. That is all. If it's in alignment with you. But adopting an idea in order to seem more than you are makes you nothing more than a fraud.

When you doom me to my fate,
my sense is that you are the one who feels doomed.
When you judge me, you're judging yourself,
and when you tell me I want a fight,
my guess is it's your own passivity that wearies you.

Things People Say

When the lava came, I quit picking up the phone. Not only because I had no words, but because of the questions and the well-intentioned support. There were even a few attacks. Because I didn't deserve to mourn, because my lifestyle was outside of the norm, therefore less real, and less painful to lose. I don't want to write an entire story about this part. It's more of a laundry list of the things people say.

The most helpful comments were the ones that didn't ask me to think, the ones that just said, I love you. Even the offers of help were confusing, offering me solutions when I wasn't yet clear on the problem. My home was still there. I could go back. Then when it was gone, I found that I still didn't have answers.

Knowing that so many friends were offering me a place to come to, to rest, did help, even if I didn't act on them. Knowing I had options gave me a place in my mind to get out of the rat maze of what do I do now. I knew there was a place to go, if I was ever ready.

How can I help? I don't know. My Aunt Merry asked me this question and instead of pressuring me to know, she figured something out on her own. She sent me a gas mask when there were none to be had on the island. And her church group sent me money.

- **"Your place is gone, stop looking back."** This one hurts and also makes me angry. Don't bother telling me no one can make me feel angry. There are times when mincing words is less than useful. I was angry because it's not up to someone else how long I spend grieving, or what it is that I grieve. Grieving is a way to honor the loving of what is gone.
- **"Why be upset when there's nothing you can do about it?"** We aren't machines — feelings are messy. I understand that if I don't feel what I'm feeling, the feelings will find another way to come out. I'd rather go through this consciously.
- **"Move on."** Thanks, I'm choosing to move through, so when it's done, it's done.
- **"What will you do now?"** I have no idea.
- **"Come to my home. You can stay with me."** Thank you.
- **"I love you."** Me too you.
- **"What did you expect would happen, living on the side of a live volcano?** The same thing you expect by living where there are earthquakes, hurricanes, cyclones, and commuter traffic. That I won't be a casualty.
- **"Will you come home now?"** I am home.
- **"You didn't lose a real house."** It was my home and as real to me as yours is to you. It was mine. I owned it.
- **"You're alive."** And?
- **"You're strong, you always rise from the ashes."** Yes, and I'm tired.
- **"I lost a dream too, you know."** This isn't a competition. I do know you lost something, that doesn't diminish my pain, or yours. Nor does it make responsible for fixing yours.
- **"Didn't you camp at Pohoiki all the time anyway?"** I bought and paid for the life I wanted. That included camping when I felt like it and having a home to return to afterwards.
- **"You've changed."** Duh!
- **"It looks like you're having so much fun in your RV. I am so jealous."** Wow.
- **"Your place was a mess."** Two steps forward, one step back. It was a work in process, if not progress.
- **"Your life was too hard. My wish for you is an easier life."** It was

hard and easy would be nice, but I loved it as it was and was working toward better.

- **"The jungle was bad for you because of the mold."** True, not helpful, but true. Sounds a lot like "I told you so."
- **"The wagon was old and should have been condemned anyway."** Whatever. Hater. It was fabulous and my guess is that I'm the only one you'll ever know who's done such a thing.

> *Lean into what you believe about me...what I believe about you...*
> *the aikido of it all. Because it's all true. Because we believe it.*
> *It is true. And because I can believe something else, this also, is true.*
> *The revolution begins at home.*
> *If you overthrow yourself again and again,*
> *you might earn the right to help overthrow the rest of us.*

Most of what was said was meant to be helpful, and I felt that. It was still too hard to field the commentary when the voices in my head had just as much to say, and more. That's why I stayed off the phone, and it's why I wrote, and posted live feed updates on Facebook. That way the people who cared about me could still know I was okay and what was happening, but I didn't have to repeat myself or become more anxious and confused.

As for the ones who weren't helpful, it was obvious they were fueled by resentment, jealousy, or thoughtlessness. Their comments say more about them than they ever did about me.

I'm going to say this as sweetly as possible. Fuck anybody who's judging me, including myself.

When somebody is judging us, they are giving us a bird's eye view of what's going on inside of their own heads. The words they choose on the outside give them away. So, if you're telling me not to feel or to be strong or whatever it is, it's you that you're talking to, not to me. It's hard, when you're in pain, to not have a knee-jerk response though.

I feel intensely. I love intensely with the understanding that by choosing to love intensely, that I could feel loss equally as intense. When I'm in the loving intensely part, I'm fully willing to take on that risk, absolutely knowing that at some point I'm going to lose and it's going to hurt like bloody fucking hell. I accept that risk until the moment when it does hurt like bloody fucking hell. And then I'm like, what was I thinking?

The bottom line is that I can't stop loving because loving is like breathing.

Through it all, I knew that you cared, and that you wanted to help. You wanted to have answers when there were none. You couldn't help but wonder what you would do in my shoes, so if I had answers, maybe they could answer the questions in your own head.

I don't have your answers. But YOU do.

SECTION THREE: AFTERMATH

CHAPTER 29:
Moved

Live feed
https://www.youtube.com/watch?v=0HB-n1jfLMA

...I've moved, now instead of hearing the jet engine roar or lava bombs of fissure 8, we've got rain and coqui frogs, and I killed a cockroach...things are getting back to normal... [laughing]

...I went to FEMA today, pushed myself and am on the verge of collapse now...I made my bed and broke into pouring sweat...stayed home instead of going out to dinner with the others...

...there are new pictures of fissure 8...I think fissure 8 could be a great euphemism. You know, like when you go ballistic, you just had a fissure 8...it's so far beyond a fissure. I read tonight it's 180 feet, which is 18 stories...two months ago it was flat...it's amazing to see this. And there's another part of my brain that says that was home, that was jungle, that was quiet. That was another life...

...tomorrow they're opening up Highway 130, which is awesome because that's the road down to Uncle Robert's, to the little bit of coastline that we have left in Lower Puna...I'm starting to accept that I'm not going home. I know it's not the same as it was but it's still mine...

...FEMA asks us what we want to do. They don't want to impose their plans on us. They want to give us an opportunity if we have already made a decision, to support that. I don't know what I want now. I feel like giving up. Like just house-sitting around the world for the rest of my life or digging in and remaining a part of this amazing community and being a part of whatever new community is being created...

...tonight, I'm on a real bed. I'm not sleeping in my minivan. I'm sprawled out. Just like I used to be in my wagon. Lily is upset. One of the dogs chased after her the other day, and even though she kind of won the battle, she scratched the crap out of him, she's still scared and pissed off at me, so she's roaming around here somewhere. I gave her some catnip, hopefully that'll do...

...I know it's probably hard to believe how loud those coqui frogs are, and that I'm going to go to sleep to it and sleep so well, and it's raining. I feel like I'm home. I feel like I'm back in my jungle, and in my gypsy wagon, I've got my kitty,

I've got coqui frogs, I've got rain, and there's no such thing as a crazy-ass fissure 8, or a lava river or lava boats...

...tonight I am going to pretend everything is still there...

Fissure 8
F8
Fate
braided lava channel
- a figure 8 -
Fate
Sign of Infinity
The Ouroboros
In all beginnings are endings
In all endings are beginnings
Fissure 8

7/7/18

This experience is stretching us all in ways you can't imagine. My body is sore with grief.

I thank Pele and the Gods of Chaos for putting something precious, my Grandma Ethel's fire opal pin, where it didn't belong, and for randomly knocking over the bag of paper clips it was hiding in so I would find it today.

My charm bracelets.

I've thought of this pin every day since this started, wishing it hadn't been left behind.

Also, in my hand are two charm bracelets.

One of them my Grandpa Harry made for Grandma Cherole during World War II while he was stationed in England. He was one of the soldiers who wrote letters to families about their fallen loved ones. When he wasn't writing letters, he made this bracelet using silver surgical pins and coins. It's been mine since my Gram promised it to me when I was three.

The other one I made to remind myself of where, and who, I've been. It has charms on it like tents, snorkel gear, microphones, and pool tables.

I also have the rings I always wore. The rest is gone. Diamonds, moonstones, and my son's first teeth. All are part of the aina now.

Pele adorned herself with my floats and sparkly things on her way down.

I was afraid at first that as I lost my things, I was also losing the memories they held. But I think they're still here, or in the memories I share with friends. Or maybe our memories grow into us and we don't need to remember anymore because they're part of who we've become.

I no longer believe that loving our things is simply materialistic. There is a richness in our relationships to our Places and our Things that we might be missing by trying to achieve such enlightenment, when in our heart of hearts, it may not be what we truly feel. 🩶

We get shamed for loving our things, as if it's not spiritual. I'd say to pretend our places or things don't matter, when they do, is anything but enlightened. It can cause a division in our soul to deny our love, even when what we loved is no longer here, be it a Person, Place, Thing, or Dream.

There are a lot of things we'd never do if we knew how they would end. But what beauty would we miss...

I want to go home. I want to hold my land and say goodbye.

My god it hurts.

CHAPTER 30:
Gone

7/11/18

Live feed
https://www.youtube.com/watch?v=XRdfAT1IVZI

...I'm already crying so it's probably not going to get better from here...
...The pond is gone...
...I spent the day crying after dealing with FEMA and the Tax Board and all these people who know that I lived there but have to question me because I lack utility bills...
...It's heartbreaking to be losing the pond. I bought my land where I did because of its proximity to the pond. Now my place is gone, and the pond is gone, and the lava is a half mile from Pohoiki...
It just seems to be taking out all of Lower Puna.
...I want to stay in Lower Puna, if any of us want to stay here, we're kind of running out of reasons why. I mean, I know that when this is over there will be new, beautiful places and it's just a matter of what do we do between now and then...
...There's no place else I want to live here, you know. I mean, I chose Puna because, well, Puna chose me, but I chose it because it reminded me of places I loved on Maui before it got so crowded...
...I don't know where to go...
...Everything is derailed...
...There are people that I only know from the pond, whose real names I don't even know. Like my friend Mango. That's it. That's all I know, is Mango. And he lived in Vacationland, and Vacationland is gone. There are a lot of people that I don't know if I'll ever even see again...
...Now it's another thing that's gone...
...I went to my friend's house yesterday. I drove down her driveway, she's near Leilani right outside of it. There are acid holes eaten through the leaves on the trees, if the trees are still green, and if they're not, they're just brown sticks...
...I just can't believe that the pond is gone...
...I don't know what to do guys. I don't know what the answer is. I don't. I'm still going through the motions of getting help from FEMA. But it's not going

to be much. It might be the RV life for me again and moving to Sayulita, Mexico…

…that's the update. A bunch of rambling sadness…

7/12/18

What do you do when you feel like you've taken a lot of hits, like, the over-the-top kind, and then something else terrible happens? When you're feeling like you're already at the end of your rope, what do you do?

I mean, how many pieces can a heart be broken into before it can't go back together again?

Lily is gone.

There's nothing left guys. No home. No land. No Lily.

I just don't see the point. I don't get it.

A few months ago, I half-jokingly said I was going to change my name to Wilhelmina and disappear on walkabout. I should have. I really should have.

Now I think I will. Because. Fuck this.

7/12/18

As I was leaving FEMA today, a gecko jumped on my arm and ran up onto my face. She wouldn't get off me. She ran across my glasses and then down my arm that was holding the steering wheel.

I've had geckos jump on me before, that's not new, but never on my face, and never to just hang out. I knew it was her. I could feel such intense energy from this little green gecko. I knew it was Lily. I hadn't said anything about her missing yet, hadn't accepted she was likely gone, but when this gecko came to me, I knew it for the truth it was.

I'm so glad I had my phone handy and was able to snap a couple of pictures. Especially when I blew them up and saw that gecko had a white stripe along its nose. Geckos don't have white noses. It was her.

I knew she was there to say goodbye. That she wished she didn't have to go. She wanted me to know that it was time for us both to move on, and that she's okay. It hurts so much to write this, and to tell it through my blurry eyes.

Even though she was there to reassure me, I could feel how scared she was too. Like palpable waves of fear rolling from her to me.

Driving on the highway as a gecko runs across my face and down my arm.

She wanted me to hold her. So, I did, all the way from FEMA to the post office, from Keaau to Pahoa. She rode that way, the entire 11 miles, until I parked, and she ran up my arm and into the vent. I never saw her again.

Geckos are, in Hawaiian legends, aumakua, and the daughters of Haumau. Pele is one of the daughters of Haumau, and it's her crater that is feeding our lava river. This is Pele's chosen home. And one of her daughters, whose name I don't remember, was related to the gecko, and to dragons. Dragons play a big role in ancient carvings around the different islands because they're part of the legend.

The magic, the medicine of gecko is transformation and new beginnings. Lily chose the gecko form intentionally. She knows I love them, and that I wouldn't be afraid, and that I'd understand both messages, that she was saying goodbye, but also to pay attention, to really smack me upside the head with, it's time for change.

Got it. Change.

7/18/18

My friend Cindy wrote this and gave me permission to share with you. Lily was an extraordinary being, I knew this. I didn't get that others knew as well. I'm so grateful it was me she chose to be with.

> "Corey, for days now, I have been meaning to reach out to you. But I haven't been able to.
>
> I want to say I know what you're going through, but my Monster was 18. And about the most traveling he had ever done was up and down his cat tree. I know it sounds weird, but I would show him Lily's picture and tell him all about this Magical cat that lived in so many places and has seen so many things.
>
> But I would think to myself it's not the time, she's mad and hurt and wide open and raw. And I didn't wanna say anything that would make you feel like I wasn't there for you, I have cried every night for Lily, I know in my heart that there is another place where souls meet again. The only thing I could do was to send my wishes up to my Monster to see if he could find her and be her friend.
>
> I know I'm super sappy, and a huge dork. But it made me smile thinking about it.
>
> Corey, take your time, decisions are never made to be set

in stone they can always be changed. Do what you want, do what you need.

Someone had mentioned that gecko do you still have it?

I myself think Lily sent you that as your next companion.

Hang in there Corey, sending you hugs and Kitty nose rubs and head bumps."

My friend Laurie created an original watercolor painting of Lily.

7/19/19

And from me, one year later…

Dear Lily, it's been one year. One year since I lost my best spooner, my best traveling companion, and my most tolerant and patient friend. You weren't my pet, I was yours.

Thank you for finding me and making me yours. My life would have been so much less without you. 🐱💜 I love and miss you so much my sweet and patient girl and am having such a hard time letting go. You deserve to rest now.

Rest in Peace, my Lily love.[8]

---

[8] For more about Lily and her cat and human friends you can visit her page on Facebook, Lily the Incredible Traveling Cat, at
https://www.facebook.com/LilyTheIncredibleTravelingCat/

7/14/18

Live feed
(https://www.youtube.com/watch?v=iKq8pG25RTg&feature=youtu.be)

...Today was a bit of a rough day. Yesterday was a rough day because I wasn't talking about it. And then this morning I just felt like I was going to explode into a million pieces if I didn't say something about it. Because it hurts so bad.

Lily is gone.

As many of you know, Lily has been my companion for a lot of years. She has traveled with me. We all know that animals don't live forever but I talked to her all the time about not being ready for her to go. She was almost 16. And she's traveled with me since 2011.

Before that we were stationary, but she's always been the perfect blend of independent but affectionate cat.

Lily was my amazing companion. She's the kind of cat who made more than one of my friends, who were confirmed cat dislikers, into cat lovers, because she was just...cool.

She rode on my lap on the airplane, she went on sailing trips, she rode around in the van at my feet. She rode in the Miata with the top down and she was Lily the Incredible Traveling Cat on Facebook.

I knew that there was danger here. But she had figured it out. In the morning, she would go out into the jungle and in the evening, she would return and spend the night here with me, spooning.

I couldn't lock her in because this is a canopy and carport I'm living in and doesn't have a floor seam. It's not enclosed. I tried putting her on the leash, but she just got tangled and couldn't use the cat box. There's a kennel here I could have put her in, but I couldn't, you know, I thought about it and I thought about my life and would I want to be put in a box to keep me safe?

You already know the answer; you know I wouldn't want to be in a box so I couldn't put her in one either.

If I had, she might not have gotten hurt. I'm not a psychic, I'm just the one who loves her.

I also went to FEMA today, and finally the County has acknowledged that I live here. Which means the Red Cross was also able to acknowledge I live here, and I got some gift cards. They're leaving soon. They only stay for three months and oh my god, it's been almost that long.

Bruce Amori took another picture straight overhead of my place and it looks like there's a wall of lava that's about 40- or 50-feet tall so my house is on a, I mean, not my house, my land, once it is surveyed, is actually on a cliff now. Apparently, I'll have an ocean view. On a cliff.

The good news is there's starting to be some posts, comments, that this is easing up, that it might be ending. And honestly, I didn't realize until now that it feels like it really was just going to go on forever.

This could end maybe, you know, this could end, and that fissure could dry up. Our lives will go on...

CHAPTER 31:
My Lily

7/20/18

Video link of Lily on the dash of my car:
https://www.youtube.com/watch?v=VUtYKfaI7Wg&feature=youtu.be

I don't want to not feel the rawness. I don't want to rise above it, be zen, or be 'enlightened.' I resent being told to move on, as if there's something wrong with me for feeling. I've been told all of my life to not feel, because what I felt was uncomfortable for someone else. Because their pain couldn't be ignored when they were in the presence of witnessing mine.

Grief honors what has passed, acknowledges what was here, who and what we loved. I don't long for a sunny-side-up kind of life. I prefer a life of *belle desordre*. I prefer my emotional plate of mixed greens over a diet of iceberg lettuce. I want the bite of endive mixed in with the softness of butter, and the sweetness of romaine.

Don't pray for me to get over my grief, or for the pain to pass more quickly. It's not what I'm asking for when I share how I'm feeling. I'm not asking for anything. I'm giving you a part of me.

If you want to offer prayers, offer the kind that gives each of us the strength to feel our lives fully, to their greatest depth and breadth. That's where our beauty is. In the unbearable lightness of being.

Only in times like this, times of great trauma and great love, are we able to stretch our fingertips to touch our own edges. To catch a glimpse of who is possible and who we are in our most silent places, our most vulnerable. In the truest sense of the word, our most awesome.

I would not ask for this pain, but I will not waste it. I won't miss this chance to see me and to meet the me I don't yet know. Lily's gift to me was the kind of love that makes this possible. To glimpse our greatness, our capacity for compassion and love...it's right here, right here in our pain.

I've grown more from pain than from any other emotion, which is completely politically incorrect.

I don't grow from pain because someone told me I would. I grow from it because I knew from the inside of it, from a very young age that I was going to learn things from the hurt that I couldn't otherwise know.

7/14/18

Live feed
https://www.youtube.com/watch?v=JUsNmQszm-8&feature=youtu.be)

...awful day...

...They went looking for Lily today and she's gone. I asked them not to tell me a lot of details. But they said that she was peaceful. It didn't look like she'd been attacked...I'm going to go with the idea that that's what happened. That she died in her sleep. They're going to retrieve her and have her cremated...

...I thought I could get through this without crying, but apparently this whole situation is just, it's, you know, it's like we're raw, and the days go on endlessly and, because there's, we don't do anything but, we don't do anything except watch the most recent update or hear about the most recent 5.0 earthquake, you know, because they're still happening all day, every day, or another collapse at the crater, or loss of another beloved place, or another home. Instead of quickly, it's death by a thousand pinpricks. Lily is a tremendous loss to me. I am so grateful that she was in my life for as long as she was...

...I knew that Lily was gone. I really did. I didn't talk about it the first day she went missing because I didn't want it to be real. I kept it to myself. That night when I went to sleep, I felt her just like she would every night, I felt her jump up on the bed and come up to spoon with me, which was what we did every night for the last fifteen years...

...But it wasn't her, she wasn't there...

...Then I looked down on the carpet and I caught a glimpse of her out of the corner of my eye. It's like, oh, there she is. But no, she wasn't there...

...We all go through this, you know, we all get attached to our animal family and they love us unconditionally and they show up for us when either nobody else does, or we feel like nobody else does. And Lily, as so many of you know who spent time with her, she was an extraordinary being....

...Jung talks about differentiation and the tension of opposites. And not to get too psychological, but you know, differentiation is the maturity and the evolution of our soul. And when we reach that place, we learn that to be in the tension of opposites means we can hold conflicting emotions and thoughts at the same time....

...Not just one or the other, not just loss, not just gratitude, but both. Both grief at losing Lily and gratitude, for having Lily, and grief at losing my land and my home and everything I had on it, and that particular dream, and still see the awe-inspiring beauty of what Pele's creating...

...we're coming up on 11 weeks and it's like one endless day...

...People are in transition and people are leaving, it's not just the loss of

places and homes, it's the loss of friendships, and the things that were our daily lives...

7/15/18

After FEMA today, which went okay, my first thought back in the van was, I need to get home to Lily. And in that one thought I realized how, for all these many years, my world has revolved around her, and I liked it that way.

The thing is, yes, we lost homes, belongings, and places special and sacred to us; and some of us lost members of our animal families. Bigger than that though, we lost a way of life, and while we will rebuild, and it may be even better, it will never be what it was. There is no retrieval from lava. What's gone is gone forever.

Anyway, when I remembered that I didn't need to get back to my tent right away for any good reason, I stopped at Maku'u Farmers' Market for fresh goat cheese, sticky sweet rice sticks, turmeric tonic, a little gift for a wee baby in Petaluma, and some flower clips for my hair. I grabbed a fresh crepe as I left and headed down to Maku'u to Beach Road in Hawaiin Paradise Park to refresh my memory of what a coastline not burning looks like.

Ending my afternoon almost as if life is normal, and the rest has been just a bad dream.

What's most exciting about change is you don't know what's around the next bend.
What's scariest about change is you don't know what's around the next bend...

CHAPTER 32:
Changing My Mind

7/17/18

It's as if she was already seeing the future. This was taken when we first moved in on Hinalo Street in Lanipuna Gardens.

I can change my mind. I can shift my perspective from loss and grief, to love and gratitude. I'm even doing it, successfully, for entire minutes at a time. Right before I go back to drowning in guilt for not making different decisions. Better decisions. Decisions that always end well and never fail.

Seriously? The things my mind comes up with when I'm not watching.

Guilt is a freaking ego trip. And human perception, my perception, is a jumbled-up tangle of things I've learned, and random other things I've heard, or read, that might not even make sense if I was to stop and really look at them.

I've no idea if I ruined my life by moving to Hawaii. Guilt says I did. I'm thinking Guilt has a screw loose. Would my life be better if I'd stayed in the Bay Area? Or moved to Mexico, or Alaska, instead of Florida, or Guam, or San Diego? If I'd never owned an RV, much less two of them? Would I still be hurting if I'd never owned land in Puna, never lived in a gypsy wagon in the rainforest, perched over my own 50-foot crater? Guilt is like, yeah, duh.

Better yet (says Guilt), I should have never traded in my corporate banking gig (a bazillion years ago) for a cocktail tray, snorkel gear, or a boat helm. I should have been content with where I was, forgotten there was a horizon, or sailboats, or mountains to climb.

Guilt would have me believe that I'm only hurting now because instead of playing the straight game I chose this zigzag of a Wander Woman odyssey that I call my life. That I broke the rules and therefore should be punished.

As if.

Would making different choices mean I never lost anyone, or failed at anything, or never made an important mistake? Would I still have my son in my life, my health, my Lily, or my home? That no one I loved would ever have died, or gone away?

The answer is no.

Because death happens, and things end. And because without the path I'd chosen, nothing else I've known would have ever been. I might be sitting here right now feeling just as sad, with just as many regrets, and more. For that matter I might not be sitting here at all. And I probably wouldn't even know you.

Yes. I've lost my home. My land. My treasures. And, at least for the time being, my son. And now my Lily. Our beloved Ahalanui. My health is precarious. I am sad. What's gone is gone.

And I wouldn't have missed this for the world.

With intense love comes intense pain.

You can love a little, so it doesn't hurt a lot when it's gone. Or you can love all the way, knowing when it ends, you're going to splinter into shards.

Then, after a while, a shiny object will catch your eye. Then another. And another. And you'll forget how much this bloody freaking hurts. You'll forget how you sat here bleeding out, and that it sometimes felt like even your fingernails were in pain. And then you'll find yourself loving again, even harder than before.

But for now, you'll just bleed.

7/18/18

I think it's totally zen to recognize we can't take things with us, and they are only material things. I think it is also totally zen to contemplate what our things meant to us, and why. Not feeling what we're truly feeling isn't about being enlightened. It's about jumping on the spiritual bypass wagon in order to appear to be something other than you are.

I respect the wisdom of leaders who acknowledge the chinks in their armor, so much more than those who deny them. They seem to forget that we can see them. That their words won't cloak what they imagine we can't see.

There is a time to acknowledge that our things did mean something to us, that it does feel like a loss. It's the difference between being in our heads and being in our hearts.

If you truly feel no sense of loss, then by all means, run with that. But if you feel loss and deny it because of how many times you've read, heard, or been told that you shouldn't care, to not feel bad because they're just places, just things, then we aren't spiritually evolving but spiritually stunting.

We are practicing guilt. Sandwiched between our ego and our humanity, as we tell ourselves that we're above yearning for our things.

I'd rather appear less evolved, than push aside my real feelings of grief. I care much less about how things look on the outside than how I feel on the inside. Because how I feel on the inside dictates my decisions on the outside.

It's only by doing this, by unraveling the pieces inside of me that, in fact, ARE attached, that I can ever hope to achieve any true sense of freedom, detachment, or enlightenment.

I'm not zen. I've lived and studied and meditated in a monastery but still I am not zen. I've got a binder full of degrees and certifications in everything from psychology to SCUBA, and I still haven't achieved that state of perfection where I don't feel the politically incorrect things I'm told an enlightened person shouldn't.

There is a consciousness to all things unto their function and form. So, to say they are just things is in complete juxtaposition. It denies quantum physics, that for every action there is a reaction.

Why must I stay positive? Life is full of positives and negatives. To only acknowledge one is to be out of balance and not real.

I hope that when I share, it suggests possibilities for exploration. That's what stories are for, and I'm a storyteller.

Our relationship with ourselves is always revealed in how we respond to others.

Sitting with each other in our pain is a skill we've forgotten about in our mindless addiction to 'being happy,' and in our incessant pursuit of 'positivity.'

CHAPTER 33:
I Love Puna Still

7/24/18

We love our Places as we love our most beloved friends and family.

I'm feeling confused tonight as Pohoiki, our last place, disappears forever.

My time on the Big Island is a drop in the bucket to my friends who've been here for decades, or whose families go back generations.

And it's confusing that even though the entire landscape has changed from lush rainforest and beautiful swimming areas, to stark, steaming lava, and jagged, lava-dripping cliffs. My head says I should just go, but I don't, because no matter what it looks like, it still feels like Puna.

There's a great something here, a Puna feeling of love and aloha of oneness with the aina no matter what it looks like. We know how it feels.

UPDATE: Pohoiki amazingly made it through the night. The parking lot and boat ramp live another day. Prayers for this to end soon.

> *Predictions of hurricane Hector making a direct hit here in a few days.*
> *Not sure my tent is up for this. Or if I am. Hector blows.*

8/17/18

> *Live feed*
> *https://www.youtube.com/watch?v=Q5YcAjHguOE&feature=youtu.be*

...I woke up because a thing was crawling on me...I fell asleep early because of the chronic fatigue, it happens...the crawly thing woke me back up...I'm glad, it concerns me that I might be sleeping through some of these events...it's baffling how I cried when the lava took my home, and my stuff, and I cried about my son, and over Lily...but none of these really important events does to me what these crawly things do...every freaking night there's one...just one...

...then I looked up and there was a slug...at the peak of the canopy, directly over my head...have I mentioned I have a slug phobia...so now I'm sitting here in the middle of the night, with all this anxiety and stress over some bugs...it's going to be slimy things that take me out...

...to get the slug I tossed salt at it until...well...you get it...

...it's time for me to not live in a tent...and to sleep with my hair up because I want to and not to make sure there aren't any crawly things in it...

...and honestly, it crushes me that I haven't heard from my son...and I'm okay, but the bugs, they wear me down...

> *What you think I'm saying says more about where you're at than it will ever say about where I am.*

7/28/18

I haven't shown you where and how I'm living. Thanks to the kindness of strangers become friends, here is my for right now home.

My tent under the trees at Jeffrey's on Maku'u in Hawaiian Paradise Park.

I have full access to the showers, kitchen, and washer/dryer. I had a TV 'til recently when the picture went out, likely due to the damp. It's messy, because that's the way I roll. LOL. But my bed is made, there's carpet covering the pallets inside, and planks to cover them as a walkway over the mud outside.

Last night I watched a wormy thing crawl up my mosquito netting and leave, and a ginormous coqui frog crawl in and back out. (My reputation must precede me). The blister beetles and cockroaches are repelled by eucalyptus oil in my diffuser. Of course, all lizards are welcome and today I was even visited by one of the sweet little chirpy brown geckos, as well as a green one, and a skink. Fly strips catch flies and these stupid little black things, and citronella takes care of mosquitos. The slugs, well, you know I've got issues with them so it's Sluggo all the way.

Basically, I'm living my jungle life. Not alone, but amongst friends (real people, not these bugs). And I've got electricity. LOL. Living the high life.

8/29/18

Oh, how my heart sings when I'm in Lower Puna.

You know, down here where the steel plates and steam vents are. Down here where the jungle was, and the lava flows.

Today, a friend helped me move my things from my friend's house in Fern Acres, into my tent down on Maku'u in Hawaiian Paradise Park. I've moved into a bedroom inside the house until I leave for the mainland at the end of September, to buy a fifth wheel and a truck.

It was such a hard thing to come to, the decision to leave. We've had four months of lava and crashing rainstorms with flash flood warnings. I've been woken up by lightning striking the tree next door, causing me to immediately think that Mauna Loa had erupted and everything we'd just endured was a waste of time because we're going to die anyway. Then multiple hurricane threats in a row with Hurricane Lane drenching us in 51 inches of rain. And my doctor saying (again) if I ever want to feel better, I need to move to the desert. The only part of this that's new is the lava, and if it hadn't taken my home, I wouldn't be making this decision. But it did. And I am. I'm leaving. For a while. For now.

Wishing I was 30 instead of 54 doesn't make it so, and I need a rest. After all the jungle and lava and rain that I've negotiated, I so hate giving in. It feels like giving up. And while I tell myself it's not, maybe it's okay if it is. How much stronger do I have to prove myself to be? When is strong enough, enough?

Anyway, back to moving day and being once again grateful that I don't always put things back where they belong. I thought I only had some furniture, a steamer trunk, and my antique wooden ammunition boxes stored at my friend's place up in Fern Acres. That was mostly true. And I'm giving most of it away if you want it.

But I found the etched Irish Crystal highball glasses that belonged to my Great Grandfather, Captain Charles White. They are not his ship's compass, or sextant, which I know are gone, but still they are something that was his. And I found a photo album. One. Maybe there will be more surprises. I'm feeling lucky. And strangely grateful to have been here for this time. Before the lava. And now. Truly epic.

To experience all of Puna and Pele and Aila'au firsthand, in their terrible strength as they bent us to the form and shape of their will.

I'm not angry at the county or state for allowing us to build in an area they knew was dangerous. I knew it was dangerous. I knew I was here at Pele's will. Heck, it was her idea for me to be here in the first place, not mine.

I was terrified when I first met my dark and mysterious little acre. But she owned me, and I was glad. What an incredible thing it was to live in a gypsy wagon in the jungle, perched over my own fern-lined crater. I'm in awe. Always was. Always.

Puna makes my heart sing. Literally. My insides humming with jungle vibes. But it's the Puna that's missing now. The Puna that's been locked away forever, either by lava, or in the interim by Civil Defense. I know she will call to me again when it's time to return.

I'll be okay. I am okay. I'm a gypsy. I don't feel completely alive when I'm inside of a house for too long. A regular house. In my gypsy wagon, or an RV, or a boat, I'm at home. Anything else feels too civilized. I'm withering. Spiraling into depression from holding too still.

I am drawn to the wild and untamed.

Drawn to my jungle.

It was a hard life. The coquis and fire ants and cockroaches and slugs and snails and rats and pigs. Sometimes more than hard. Like my mind could break against its impenetrable countenance. It was muddy and frustrating and daunting and so freaking wild and beautiful that no matter how near to the brink it sometimes took me, the minute I turned down my street toward home, all of me began to smile. I was knit together again, my insides united. So much joy in so much beauty. I was as happy as if I was in my right mind. I was.

God. It was magnificent.

Mahalo for this experience. For Puna. For this community who showed the world what aloha means.

I love you.

7/28/18

To comfort us for our losses we are told that what we lost are just things. That we are alive, and safe, and that's what counts.

Having left most everything behind I can tell you it's a strange feeling. It's a hard feeling.

Standing at the donation center, volunteers asking, "What do you need?" Evacuees wandering through the tables in a daze, wondering, "What do I need?" Q-Tips, deodorant, yes, a towel...so much of what we have we don't think about but are the things that make our daily lives doable.

And the rest? The treasures, the heirlooms, the keepsakes? I can live without them. I am living without them. Once upon a time, I too said, they're just things. I have a different understanding now it's all gone. That some of the things weren't just things. We'd spent time together. They carried memories for me. They were a physical representation of a moment in time.

There is a strange freedom in losing my things to the lava. Things hold us, even drag us down with what, or who, they represent. If you don't believe me, try going through some of your own boxes. The reason so much clutter doesn't get cleared is for this very reason. Our things take on a life of their own, by being in relationship with us.

Our things hold a place for us. And our things hold us in place. Not having them does something to the psyche. Maybe even our soul. I'm free floating. I've received this strange gift, which is to find out who I am without my things to define me, my things to reflect to me who I've been.

I believe there is a consciousness to everything, according to its function and form. A treasured doll from childhood doesn't have the life of a plant, or pet, or of us. But way down in there, it had a life with us, and now that life is gone.

It's okay to mourn this.

CHAPTER 34:
Self-Help Parrot

If...

- I'd stayed house-sitting for Steve and Keith
- Mana had stayed
- Sean had stayed
- Joe and Angie had worked out
- I'd built instead of cleared
- I'd waited until I felt better
- I'd bought a boat instead
- I'd bought a teardrop trailer and towed it around the mainland with my Miata
- Jeremy and Katana had stayed
- Laura had stayed
- Kalani had worked out
- Margaret had stayed
- Raj hadn't given me the wagon
- Mitchel hadn't helped so much
- Mac hadn't built the platform
- I hadn't taken my stuff out of storage
- I hadn't bought the generator
- I hadn't shipped my stuff here
- I hadn't bought all that furniture
- I'd spent more time planning
- I hadn't gone to the pond
- I hadn't posted on Craigslist
- I hadn't broken my ankle
- I'd never moved to Hawaii in the first place

Then what, exactly?

I'd be living a different life, with just as many chances of something happening. I made the decisions that I did, based on the life I wanted to lead. It didn't work out as planned. There are no guarantees. Playing it safe would have kept me no safer than it kept those who've been through fires, floods, earthquakes, hurricanes, or car accidents.

I took risks and I lived a glorious adventure for a while that I'll never forget or regret. Regardless of how much it hurt in the end. I won't talk myself out of the experiences by using politically correct words. It is what it is. I am who I am.

To live the life you dream of, you have to turn away from the voices around you. You must learn to walk the line between trusting the voices in your head, and not believing everything you think.

7/29/18

It's no use to impose an enlightened directive upon myself if it's not how I feel. I've talked about this before, about how reading about enlightenment doesn't make us enlightened. It's purpose is to inspire us to become so.

What we are offered is the opportunity to be aware of and to reach for such a thing. But there are no shortcuts to enlightenment. We've got to feel it to know it. And when you offer us advice you're not actually living on the inside; we can feel it. I can feel it. Then who I'm really imposing upon is myself. I'm not allowing my inner being to learn and be imperfect. Instead I'm being shiny on the outside but on the inside, I am an emotional cripple.

It's not about faking it 'til I make it. It's about being as authentic and close to the truth of who I am as I can be. Only then can I reach for the next rung and hope to remain without falling off. Or stop feeling like a fraud who's about to be 'found out.'

Do I think that by appearing to be enlightened, by saying what I've read as if it's how I live my life, rather than how I'm telling you to live yours, that I'll magically become who I want you to think that I am? That by saying the right things, that when this life ends and I reach the other side, that my guides will be there with gold stars, cheering me on for appearing to be wise?

No way. They're going to shake their heads and ask me why I wasted so much time pretending to know, when I could have been actively pursuing knowledge instead. Then they're going to send me back down here to do it again.

Being human hurts. It's messy. It's confusing. It's a game of endings and beginnings. I'd love to be one of those people on stage, guiding you toward your own enlightened truths. But I can't, if it means I must appear to be perfect. That might serve you for a short time, until you became disillusioned with my words, and I became disillusioned with myself.

We are here to be human. If I believe I'm more enlightened or am in a race to be an old soul, all I'm doing is indulging in spiritual narcissism. Ego seeks attention by appearing to know. Spirit seeks to just know and doesn't care how it looks while it's getting there.

When I open my mouth to *tell*, it's me who needs to listen. When I open my mouth to *share*, I'm allowing spirit to flow through to guide what wants to be heard. It's not for me to parrot someone else's words without having lived them out loud for myself and made them into my own. And then, only if I'm being asked.

Except of course in one of my essays, where I can say whatever I want and you can choose to read it, or not.

I don't believe that crying makes us weak.
I think to acknowledge how we feel takes extreme bravery.
What if it feels like too much and we drown? Or what if it makes others
uncomfortable? Or what if I look a fool? Or what if I don't care about those things and
instead of getting over it, I go through it? What could happen then, if I were to go into my
own darkness and make it through to the other side? Who might I then be?

7/30/18

It's hard to accept the things that come easily, as things that matter. It's even harder to understand that because it's easy for me, it might not be for you. And when it's easy for you, it may not be for me. We aren't all here for the same reasons.

For things to reveal themselves to us, we need to be ready to abandon our views about them, and about who we think we're supposed to be.

With a background in psychology it's very easy for me to get all up in my head with diagnosis and analysis.

Finding a balance between what we think and what we feel is a lifelong pursuit, if evolution is your goal.

Staying in my head alleviates the need to feel. It means I can point at a sickness in our society and shake my head as I pretend that because I can observe it, I am above it.

After reading the books, watching the videos, and attending the workshops, I know the right things to say. That's how I lived for a long time, being politically correct in my emotions in order to hide the pain that I was in. My recovery and healing were built on castles in the air. Inside I was dying. So I stopped lying to me, and to you.

Appearing to be positive when I'm confused, or hurt, or sad, is spiritual narcissism. And it's everywhere I look. People up in their heads thinking someone else's thoughts instead of dropping the 12 inches into their hearts. It's the vulnerable and scary thing to do but it's path that leads to sanity. It took me a long time to figure this out. That's okay.

Life isn't a race. It's not about getting there (where?) first, being an old soul, a victim to your empathy, or any of the other current buzzword status titles. Young souls are people too, and just as important. It's not about comparing my insides to your outsides, or your reading something in a book then stringently pasting it over your heart.

Comparing. Competing. Contrasting. Knowing others have it worse.

We should be grateful.

None of this diminishes our pain, just the space we allow ourselves to feel it in. We mean well but please think about what you're saying. Should we feel better because others feel worse?

I don't know if I can do it all the time, but for now, I'm willing to allow myself this kind of space.

I'm a human who has just suffered a succession of blows and have decided that being stoic doesn't serve me. The pain needs to be expressed before it takes up permanent residency in my soul.

CHAPTER 35:
Gratitude

8/1/18

Warning: deep gratitude expressed below, and I feel a little silly doing it out loud. But here goes. Because balance matters.

With the heartache there is also joy.

It's been 13 weeks and here we are.

My friend, Imago recently shared her reflections on her new 'normal.' This is a glimpse into mine.

My personal 'flying fridge' that I caught at the Hub.

What more could I need?

Yesterday, I stopped by the Hub to say thank you for all they've done. Pu'uhonua O Puna rose so fast for us.[9] At a time of shattering and fragmentation, when so much was happening at once, when there was so much loss of home and gathering places and neighborhoods. You created a new one for us. Mahalo for being the heart of our community at a time

---

[9] https://www.facebook.com/puuhonuaopuna/

when our hearts were breaking. Thank you to all your dedicated volunteers, your boundless aloha, and for so quickly responding to our community's needs. You gave us a place to go for information, supplies, hot meals, hugs, love, and friendship.

And, thank you April and Kevin and Donovan for all you did for everyone living in the parking lot at the evacuation center. Thank you Brandy for making sure Lily always had the kind of food she needed. Thank you April, for the use of the massive carport tent, my carpeted pallet floor, the wardrobe, the deluxe blow-up bed, the feather mattress, the lamp, the ginormous wine glass, for taking care of Lily, for inviting me to tag along to our current living place, and for letting me borrow your dog when I was sad.

And to everyone who moved me from the evac center and set up my living space. And to Jeffrey for inviting us in.

Yes, I've lost a lot, we all have. But if I look at only that, I will feel only that. When I look at what I have, it's not a 'yeah, but.' It's simple 'YEAH.' Here I am, dry and comfortable enough, amongst friends in Hawaii.

So much has come to me, and I think the only thing I've asked for was ice and tarps way back when. So, thank you Pastor Brian, for helping us up in the parking lot, starting with your daily trips to bring us ice. Then you went on, giving dozens of people shelters and emergency kits. Every single day. Thank you for the popsicles.

This list goes on for a long time, to include Ikaika, Philip, John, Bruce, Dane, Harry, Mick, and Ryan (off the top of my head) for your amazing photography and for keeping us accurately informed since day one. To Dragon sister, Oshi, and Mouse, and Frannie, who I met through the Hub or Hawaii Tracker. How our experiences with the lava strengthened friendships, like it has with my Seastars, who are too many to name.

And to my friends, here and out there, Mahalo. When I fell apart you kept track of the pieces.

CHAPTER 36:
In Between

8/2/18

I'm wondering about the place in between. Between the extremes of either/or and black and white. But especially, I'm wondering, is there a place in between the question of, do I stay, or should I go? There must be.

I'm so tired. And as much as I work at being grounded and keeping my focus, it doesn't stick. My attention strays, and once again I'm swept away. How could it be otherwise when a burning river of lava is rolling across our Lower Puna landscape?

That's energy, man, it's not just happening to the planet, it's happening in our bodies, our psyche, and our soul. We are caught up in the flow. We are part of the aina, and she is part of us.

For too long we've behaved as if nature and human nature are exclusive of each other rather than being intertwined and interacting.

Because it matters. Energy matters.

Yes. I said that.

Think about the places you've been. They all have their own feel. Their own personality.

They are alive. They are Matter. So are we.

I feel differently in Hawaii than I feel in other places. When I fly in and look down at the water, I get this sensation—as if I'm re-attaching an important part of my own body, without having known until that moment, it was even gone. It's always been this way. Since my first touchdown in 1981 on Oahu, coming to Hawaii has always felt like coming home.

Coming back to me.

Looking through my archway toward my ohia rainforest from
my platform. See my photo essay at
www.coreyhale.com/gallery.

The first time I saw my acre of Puna jungle though, I felt slightly different. It was more like, 'oh hell no'... this was some seriously tangled, overgrown, dark-ass rainforest jungle, and way beyond my pay grade. It felt old and alive and I was frightened and intrigued. My eyes got big and I looked away. My heart jerked and I went in search of something easier. Something more manageable.

I investigated other areas of Puna, but I kept coming back to here. To Hinalo Street in Lanipuna Gardens. After a month of trying to forget about her, I played a game of *House Hunters* in my head. I asked myself how would I feel if someone else lived there instead of me? Mic drop. I made an offer and it was accepted the next day.

Then we tried to get on the land. We walked around what we could get to and tried to force our way through what we couldn't. The waiwea (strawberry guava) were too close in the front and the cane grass too thick on the sides. The back was a 20-foot pile of trees that had been cut to build my neighbor's driveway, which ran behind my land. Plus, there were rifts and small ravines. By the final day of inspection, I was having serious doubts. I mean, what was I thinking? I'd been a wanderer my entire life. Now I was going to OWN land? And do what—have a freaking lawn??? And then?

My forehead was a wrinkle of confusion.

Finally, on the last day of inspection, we just crazy forced our way in... we used machetes...and that's when I fell in love. Game over, do not pass go, do not collect $200 kind of IN LOVE. I was in. Before me lay my crater. There were thick, tangled vines hanging all around, a massive canopy of trees so thick that light could barely filter through, and two majestic granddaddy ohia growing up from inside of the crater to tower over it all.

I'll forever remember that moment. It involved butterflies in my stomach, and jungle vines weaving their way into my heart, as they wrapped themselves around and inside of me. Like they'd been waiting for my return. And I was in. I was owned.

There was no question. I belonged.

Now it's all been returned to Pele. And still, I am IN LOVE. But what do I do? There's another hurricane headed our way. It happens every year and usually misses us. But I'm in a tent. And I'm tired. And I don't have as much trust as I once did.

Some days I'm overflowing with love and gratitude and on those days, I think, okay, I'm okay now. I'm staying. On other days my heart hurts and I cry. And I think, no, I've got to go.

There's just got to be an in between.

Can you have place karma?
Like an energetic location or relationship with the archetypes there
and it's only by being there that you can work it all out? Or is it a sacred contract?
Who or what embodies the place consciousness?
More soul and spirit from the great amoeba in the sky?

CHAPTER 37:
Home Inspection

Today, I meet with FEMA for my 'home' inspection. In my case, this means sitting with a stranger in the church parking lot and listing all my stuff.

I've got a notebook I've been writing in as I remember. At first, I tried to be organized with categories. What it's become is pages and pages of random and rambling 'stuff.'

For an off-grid jungle girl I had accumulated a lot of stuff. Power tools. My chainsaw, weed whacker, Honda generator, portable inverter, building materials, tarps, awnings, and electronics. Then there's the antiques and a ton of art supplies. The kitchenware. The towels, blankets, spices, CDs, DVDs, camping stuff, portraits, pictures, baby books (mine, my son's, and my Gram's), herbs, essential oils, jewelry, books, pottery.

Grandma Ethel's knitting needles.

Christmas decorations. Sean's first tooth. My great-grandfather, Captain Charles White's ship's compass.

Two boat port-a-potties. A dozen five-gallon buckets, paint cans, rollers.

My gypsy wagon. My platform. My outdoor shower. Hoses, nozzles, organic pesticides, and gardening tools. My Girl Scout badges.

My marble countertops. My wrought-iron outdoor furniture. The hot water heater, gas cans, and propane tanks. My wind chimes.

The refrigerator magnets, the journals, the tiaras, the Crocs, and my Crayons. My coloring books. My cookbooks.

All the shells and rocks I've gathered from all the places I've been. I'm 54. That's a lot of rocks. That's a lot of places.

These are the challenging days. Going over what was, when all I want to do is forget and look ahead. Being sad that so many of my things were in boxes, waiting for my about-to-be-built 'big' house, so they could come out and play.

All the things I'd planned to do with them around my land. Little pathways and surprising places to sit and contemplate, alone or with friends. All the beauty. There's no place to itemize those things.

It's all still in me. My land may be black with lava, but in my head it remains in vivid color.

> They've lifted the evacuation to Leilani.
> Pohoiki is open to those who can make the hike in.
> I'm crying so hard that I can't go home to Lanipuna Gardens and that this has ended.
> And that we can pick up the pieces, and that we can never go back.

> There's another hurricane headed our way.

8/18/18

Sitting at a bar in Kailua-Kona, Willie K is piping through the speakers. There's a perfect, ocean breeze. People all around wearing nice clothes— they match and don't have any holes. Not a dreadlock in sight. No mud. Mai Tais are $14. I've got an ice cold Cube Libre in front of me.

I'm a poet whose medium is prose.

I'm listening—while I swim in the pool, remembering the pond and hearing echoes of our voices—to the people and to the pieces of me as they shuffle around in confusion. My pieces aren't sure where they belong anymore. The lava pieces, and the health pieces that make grocery shopping an event, and the pieces that lived and worked on the other islands for all these many years.

The me who was a deckhand and sometimes first mate on Windjammer, who ran around the 68-foot schooner like I had a prehensile tail. The me who used to put kawa kawa (fish) in Willie K's tip jar when he played at the Pioneer Inn in Lahaina Harbor. Him in his tie-dye shirts, killing it on his 12-string guitar, his wild island hair flying as he effortlessly hit those high C notes. I would beg him to sing *Sweet Lady of Waihole* by Brudda Waltah, and he'd usually say no (not because he didn't like the song, but because I always asked), until he realized I wasn't going to stop asking.

There are pieces of me who house-sat on Kauai, and who played tourist at the now defunct Club Lanai. The me's who were a snorkel instructor, an air balloon flyer, and a cocktail waitress. The party animal who rode her bike three miles through the dark of early mornings, waiting for car headlights to illuminate the road ahead so I could see where I was going. The me who, at the end of a day of snorkel instructing, sailing, BBQ-ing, and bartending, drank the beers, tipped the kawa kawa, played the liar's poker, then rode those three miles back home to climb 11 flights of stairs, bike on my shoulder, to a one-bedroom condo I shared with four people, where I would plop down on the green vinyl couch I called home.

Reality is, guys, I'm meant for that life. It's me. But this life I was having has been me too. I longed for a forever home. Almost as much as I long for the open road. Sigh.

Where will my pieces land? Are we ever totally willing to see what's true about ourselves? Can we be willing to be more than a sum of the parts we were given, and truly allow ourselves to be who we are?

And, if we can, how do we know when it's happened?

CHAPTER 38:
Consumption

9/4/18

This was sunrise on 5/3/18. It seemed like the sky was already burning. We had an idea of what was to come, but no idea of the magnitude, or impact, or how much redder the sky was going to get.

Waking up to the sky on fire not knowing the eruptions would begin later that day.
(Photo by Yvonne Baur)

Five months and still we wait, and while we wait, I wonder.

Is Puna up for consumption? Does being enlightened entitle you to trespass? Do dollars qualify you for more?

Just because I can do something doesn't mean I should.

I'm not Hawaiian. I grew up in the forests and fields of Northern California, where my family (aunts, uncles, cousins, grandparents) would camp together for the summer. As a kid I remember running through the mountain woods at Lake Pillsbury and stumbling across an outdoor church. Not really a church, just a small, square frame, made of narrow trunks of madrone notched together like Lincoln Logs. It felt like a chapel because there were three split log benches facing forward toward a roughly made podium.

Kicked out of Sunday school when I was four, for asking the wrong questions, I didn't know how church worked, or what people did in them that didn't get them into trouble. Sometimes I'd sit on one of the benches and try to do what I thought might be praying. Or I'd stand at the podium, looking at the benches and wondering what I was supposed to feel.

I imagine it wasn't all that hidden or secret from the local community, but to me it felt mysterious and enchanted. I couldn't wait every year to return to run up the steep mountain path. I'd run until I had a stitch in my side, weaving and wandering through the trees until I'd find it again. And when I did, I'd sit quietly, wondering why it was there, and if this was what Church felt like. I didn't know then that spiritual was different than religious, nor did I understand that what I might be feeling was reverence and awe.

How it felt to be there has never left me in the time in between.

I feel something like this when I consider what's behind the barricades of Civil Defense. But the feelings are bigger. Way bigger. I want to walk into Lower Puna, and I want to whisper. I want to listen to this new place that Pele and Aila'au have made of the place where we used to be.

I want to listen for the new voices. I want to see what has changed. I want to bear witness. I want to hear who is there. Will the spirit of what was there remain, and if so, whose voice will be the strongest, the one that was, or the one that is? Or have the two, while we've been sitting here waiting, already begun merging, one becoming indistinguishable from the other?

I want to walk quietly, hearing the tephra crunch beneath my feet like icy snow, toward the new pond at the boat ramp. I want to walk down the empty, leaf-strewn road, and out onto the new black sands.

Will I feel what I felt all those years ago in the woods? The same confusion about how to do it right? I think I'm supposed to chant but I don't know the words. But I could speak. I could say, I'm here to meet you and to learn to begin to know you. I'm honored to be here with you in this moment in this sacred place and space. I am in awe.

I want to quietly know these Places.

And I feel conflicted. I'm enraged by some of those who've gone in before and who've snuck in to take. To take pictures, to take something that's pristine and sacred and I'm afraid is being missed in these first moments of hello. In exchange for the chance to be the first to consume.

Our places are not for consumption. I owned my land but had confusion about that too.

How do you own a piece of a planet? And why must it be owned and why must some take more than they need, just to say they have? And why can they lock the gates with us on the outside? And, after all of the gates, why do those who've been locked out want to now put up gates of their own?

I agreed to tend to my land knowing my time was short in comparison to hers. Kilauea is Pele's home. It was at the whim of Pele that I was here at all. I want this still. And I want to overhear tourists say, "Let's be here now" instead of what I heard too often—"Hurry up, let's take some pictures so we can go to the next place to take some more." Let's consume. Let's take. Pictures.

It's not the photography or the desire to see that are at issue. There are so many who've gone in for us, who've documented, and seen for us. Who've taken pictures so that the rest of us could see. You can feel their love and connection and respect.

It's that our Places need us to be present for them too. They want to be with us. For us to look and to see who they are. For their sake and ours. Not just dirt to use or trees to cut. They want to meet us too.

We can only perceive that which perceives us. So, when everywhere we look, we think we own, and it's ours to do with as we will, as if it has no life of its own, who in the meantime, is perceiving us? And who will be the first to disappear? Who is already gone?

I want to know this new Place before it is made quiet by the voices yelling loudest.

I want them to leave Puna alone.

Thoughts matter. Thoughts are things. Things matter. Things aren't just things.
Bottom line is, if thoughts are things, then things do matter. All things.

9/6/18

I usually don't know what I'm going to say until it's written.

This happens a lot in the middle of the night. It happened a few nights ago at 2 a.m. I grabbed my phone and I tapped it out, one finger at a time. I wasn't sure I should publish it until I read it aloud to a friend, who started crying.

There is tension. Anger. Resentment.

It's a difficult time. An in-between time. For those still here, for others who've evacuated off island, and for the tens, and maybe hundreds of thousands of you around the world who've been watching with us.

What do we feel in a disaster in slow motion? What do we do with the love that can turn to anger without us even knowing it's happened because it hurts so much? How do we not lash out? How do I drop my thoughts from my head into my heart, when all I want to do is go home to a place that no longer exists? What do we do with the tears we've been saving up for the day when we get to go home? What if we never go home at all? What happens to those tears then?

And how do we find the strength to go about our days when our attention is split, and a part of our hearts has wandered off to permanently dwell beyond the barricades?

By knowing that we can. By paying attention to the words and to the feelings. By listening for the metaphors. Especially when I wake up with anger and frustration running me before I've even opened my eyes. And sometimes I fail. I forget to pay attention, to remember how much strain I've been under, and that my normal, isn't.

On those days I hear it in my voice, and in my words. I point my finger. I say, this is the problem. They are to blame. And I feel the anger rumbling under my hood. If I'm not paying attention, I say things in ways that hurt. Then I hurt. Then I double-down, trying harder to pay better attention.

It's tough. Anger. But it's a feeling, just like love. And it's an important stage to acknowledge in our grief. If I don't find a way to move through it, the feelings can only become aggression. Or depression. Or road rage. Or a heart attack.

So, what do we do with the feelings?

There's a scarcity that's been created in Puna that's false. Scarcity fuels fear and fear fuels anger. But our island is still here for us. Our places are here. We miss them. We want to go home. We don't know what to do with it all. We forget the ouroboros; that in all endings are beginnings, and in all beginnings are endings.

I don't know what to do with it all.

Except to lean away from the anger and into the love. We're either in this alone or we're in this with each other. It's our choice. It's a choice. It's my choice. It's yours.

Last night I dreamt that someone stole my Grandma Cherole's charm bracelet. I woke up so sad. It took me a while to remember it was just a dream.

There are other things I'm sad about that I wish I could also wake up from. Sometimes bad things just happen. And all we can do is watch.

9/18/18

I got it right between the eyes today.

When I woke up, I wished I hadn't. I wished I'd continued sleeping. At least for a little while longer.

I don't want to feel right now. I'm tired. Too weak in my health and body to easily combat the tidal wave of emotions that are waiting just on the other side of okay.

Because most days I am. Okay. And I think it's permanent. I notice and wonder and think, why are others still in pain?

Because I am. Because it comes in waves. Some days the waves are calm, I know they are there, but they don't reach me. And then there are stormy days when it's all I can do to keep from being swept away by the riptide. The rogues. The ones that come upon me without warning. And on those days, I fight just to breathe.

Puna is in a struggle. Between people and politics and money and scarcity. And ownership. And entitlement. And by the threat of gentrification.

The world is a wonderland. Not a theme park. The cost of admission is supposed to be more than the price of a ticket. It's supposed to include honor and respect and attention with intention. The lava is not just another ride to get in line for. The planet is more than another Disneyland.

When it hurts like this it feels like it will never end.
That I will always be the walking wounded.
I don't think that's trauma's true purpose.
I think it's meant to shake us out of complacency.
Even when what we had before wasn't a walk in the park.

CHAPTER 39:
Outside

10/5/18

It's been a gift to be inside four walls while I considered my options.

For my last couple of island days though, I MUST be outside. No indoor plumbing or ice makers.

Just me in my van. Missing my Lily cat terribly, missing going home to my jungle so much, missing my friends at Warm Ponds, my gypsy wagon, missing the sweet little life that had finally gotten its groove on.

I know it's superstition, but I feel like I said, 'I've finally got my feet beneath me,' one too many times back then. Like I jinxed it. Ridiculous, I know.

The Big Island of Hawaii, especially the Puna district, is wild and it can be a harsh place of contradictions and extremes. Off the top of my head this year: over 18,000 earthquakes a month for more than three months. Lava eruptions that swept over our homes, and most of our beloved places, claiming more than 13 square miles. Throw in a couple of hurricanes and tropical storms—Lane dropped fifty-one inches in just two days according to our backyard rain gauge—and that's our home. My home. Where I feel most alive. Even when I'm sick.

Except my home is gone and I'm going away. I'm longing for the desert as I've never longed before. I want calm. I want a blank terrain. I want an environment that doesn't challenge me. I want a lack of mud. I want to look out and not see a tangle of trees. I want to not chase frogs for a while.

My heart is heavy as I say another goodbye in a long line of goodbyes this year. Yes, I'll be back. I always come back. Even with all that's missing, my sweet little life is still here. Around the corner, in a friend's familiar face, and in the conversations that always, always return to us remembering the before, during, and after of the lava.

It's just, so much has changed. Inside and outside and beside the sides I've yet to see. I'm just not a house dweller. I like to visit them. Sometimes I like to stay in them for a while. There's no denying they make life easier. But they also kill something in me.

So tonight, I'm camping out in Puna, here on the lava, not THE lava, just some lava in a field of wild orchids and weeds and ferns. With my doors open, and the warm and fragrant tropical night air for walls.

I continue to obsess over maps and pictures in the hope of finding it's still there.

10/7/18

Just came across a notebook. The entry for 5/3/17: I got an offer on my property. My body gave a resounding NO, and that I needed to wait to make any decision until end of summer.

I didn't sell. And my life imploded by end of summer. My son. Then watching the fires in Sonoma County, where I grew up, and had just returned from. I watched online, all night, for days, as so many of my friends lost their homes, and as our beloved, iconic places were consumed.

I returned to Puna to find my car was totaled. I was betrayed. And a bunch of family crap happened.

And then January came. New vehicle. New plan. Peace and contentment set in like I've rarely felt. I won my disability hearing. I was finally going to build a big, open, Puna-style house. With indoor plumbing.

Then, exactly one year from that journal entry of 5/3/17, where I turned down the offer for my land, 5/3/18 happened. Lava and loss happened. So much loss heaped upon itself.

I guarantee that when I wrote those things down, I couldn't have imagined in a bazillion years the ride I'd soon be on. Or that through it I'd find an even, deep place of peace and contentment, or that the fires that burned in lava and family and flame would be the very thing I needed in order to heal the wounds I thought were gone, but had continued to drive me. Or how our community would rally, or how many lifelong friends I'd begin to know.

Or that amidst the chaos, I would find my voice and be able to write what I've been waiting to write since I was six-years old.

I thought I'd be on a cool, fun adventure, something with rainbows and unicorns.

That must be what's next.

My bubble got popped.
Maybe that needed to happen so I could get a bigger bubble.
Being between bubbles sucks.

7/30/19

I Didn't Mean To

I didn't mean to stay in Truth or Consequences (T or C) for more than a few months, just enough time to get my feet beneath me and formulate my next plan. I've been here almost a year now, through freezing cold temps, and a hailstorm that totaled my Miata with stones over an inch and a half in size. Then sweltering heat of 100 degrees or more that blew out my air conditioner and made me melt.

But it was easiest.

When I moved to Puna, it was supposed to be my last move. I pulled all of me in in order to adapt to the jungle, and the rain, and to living in a village, on an island that offered limited resources. I committed so fully that something in me crossed over. My former life of cross-country travel, through city freeway mazes in fast cars, no longer felt second nature to me.

Of course, it wasn't this alone that changed me. Being sick, dealing with brain fog, and chronic fatigue and pain, and the grief that came with losing my abilities to do the work I loved, all added to my narrowing world, and escalating anxiety.

Then the lava came, and the daily onslaught that chipped away at our homes and neighborhoods. Having no choice other than to live in the moment, and to be grateful for our small village that even in upheaval offered a sense of safety and security because we were in it together.

But then there was nothing left. I was too sick to start again and even if I wasn't sick, having to wait to see if the lava would cool, if it would be possible to build upon again, or if the county would even let me. So, I left. I've traveled my entire adult life. It didn't take a lot of thought to know where to go and how to do it.

Arriving in Phoenix to purchase my RV and a car wasn't a new thing. I've done it before. Things fell into place quickly, but the culture shock, the freeways, the rapid movement of everything, and the sheer enormity of all people hit me like a brick wall. I felt exposed, unsure, and so I chose to return to T or C, knowing I had friends, and knowing there was a familiar place to park. Knowing that it was the kind of slow that I could handle. I could go back into my cocoon. I was already goo. How my pieces were being held together, looking back, I don't know. I was a shell. Shell shocked.

I lost track of days. I filled them with making my RV into a home with the help of the Dollar Store, gifts from friends, and a lot of deliveries from Amazon Prime. I made healthy meals, as healthy as was possible from the shelves of our only store in town, Walmart. But even that helped because it kept things simple. I needed simple.

It was my new normal. The normal created from no longer being tethered to my things, or a place, or to my son, who was still not a part of my life. Who was I? What was I going to do now?

It wasn't awful. It was exciting, engaging. I thought of all the places I hadn't been, places still on my bucket list. The Alcan. Lobster in Maine. My friend Missy's organic farm in New York. All the parks I hadn't been to yet. It's only now that I can see how empty I was then, a permanent deer in headlights. Grasping at things familiar to me from before. Gathering pieces of me into my lap.

I was alone. I had time to unthink. To stop thinking. To unravel even further than had already happened in Puna as we watched it disappear. To wonder. What now?

My brain wasn't entirely empty. It had this book in it. I was writing it in my head, reflecting but still not understanding that it was emptiness staring back at me in the mirror. I could hear a lot of words; the words hadn't been taken. More space for the words.

My return to Puna in January 2019 was the exclamation point on the permanence of what was changed. My heart lives in Puna. And the places that I miss and went back for aren't there, but my memories are.

I'm still fragile. My son, who came back into my life in December 2018, says no, that I'm *frageel,* his way of saying that he doesn't accept this as my permanent space, because he knows how strong I am. He reminds me.

I won't ever be who I was. And I don't know that this is a bad thing. I've gained a greater respect for the role that trauma plays in our lives. I don't wish trauma upon anyone, but trauma happens. What I wish for is for positivity to make way for what trauma has to teach us. There's no better way to find out who you are than to watch how you respond to it. To feel it pull you into darkness and sorrow and confusion, into chaos, and to continue to observe as you navigate your way through.

I'm more of who I was before I got sick. I lost a lot of faith in myself when I lost my ability to interact with the world in the ways I always had. Head on, bull by the horns, make it or break it. That was anything but being in the aikido of it. I'm finding another way to be alive, through my words. Less fearful of the future, or that I'll not be able to take care of myself. I lived in the jungle. I lived in a tent in a parking lot. I lost most of my stuff, my home, the things that I felt defined me, that held me in place, kept me intact.

I'm still me.

I'm a travelin' fool.
I was born under a wandering star and
sometimes I get mighty homesick.
Home is where my suitcase is.
I will never not wander again.
I'm a train writer. An RV writer. A boat writer.
I can't help but write when I ride.

SECTION FOUR:
THE DESERT

CHAPTER 40:
Phoenix Rising

10/11/18 **Travel Day HNL -PHX**	10/12/18 **Day 1**	10/13/18 **Day 2**
On the plane in Oahu— opened a magazine and there is Puna, the Hub, Ikaika, and our lava river. So strange to see it like it's somewhere else. Our new normal.	*First day in the desert— overwhelmed and relieved as I'm hearing there are flash flood warnings on the Big Island.*	*I think I found my Miata today*
Excited about my new adventure.	*Anita's place is nice - indoor plumbing and everything.*	
10/14/18 **Day 3**	**10/15/18** **Day 4**	**10/16/18** **Day 5**
GPS routed me onto the beltway today—thought I was going to die.	*I think I found my RV - it looks like Mauna Kea and Mauna Loa on the back, with dolphins. It's bigger than I'd planned.*	*I decided. Yes. The RV is mine!!!! I drove it today and it's not hard at all.*
I miss eye contact. You can see people trying to control every detail to distract themselves from feeling. You can see them hiding behind their own eyes. It makes me want to run.	*I bought the Miata. I think it will look great with the RV.*	*Oh, my dear frantic PTSD-riddled system, it's time to feel new thoughts. Chasing after peace and ease is missing the point. That's not how this works. So sit down and STFU.*
	Sit. Down. Breathe. You. Are. NOT. In. Danger.	

10/17/18 Day 6	10/18/18 Day 7	10/19/18 Day 8
Went to Ross today, bought totally cute red Keds.	Today I discovered bobby pins. All of my life I've been at the whim of my hair, patting things into place and hoping they'd stay.	I had a blast at Cabela's, the adult adventure store. Then got in the Miata and…no service. No GPS. All of my maps from AAA are back in the RV. So now I'm going to die.
I've learned to swear at WAZE in words I only know because I made them up once I ran out of the regular ones.	Found the eighties channel.	Stopped at Ross again (be still my heart) and came out with four very large bags. Because, yeah, starting over.
	Will I ever not miss the pond…	

CHAPTER 41:
Reflection

Almost time to go day.

Seven years ago, today, I arrived in Phoenix, with Lily, where I traded my truck for an RV.

It was 2011, I went into descent...down the rabbit hole, where I spent time with Tweedle-Dee and Tweedle-Dum, the Cheshire Cat, Caterpillar, the Queen of Hearts, and the Mad Hatter, to name a few. Of course, these are just the pseudonyms for the real cast of characters, because really, none of it was really real at all.

Not a hallucination. Not a dream (or nightmare). Nope. Something far stronger, more sinister, and more pervasive. My own perceptions, which are neither true nor false. They are merely choices we make, about which details to pay attention to, and which actions we choose to take, based on believing what we are thinking.

I can't help it. We can't help it. If we can't believe our own thoughts, what good are they? They shape our world. They give us something to hold onto. And, in the moment, what we are thinking is as true as anything else. Just don't fall into the trap of believing some things never change. Bottom line is, the only thing constant in life IS change.

All things changed for me that year. Sean was 18 and living in St. Louis with his bio dad. I'd finished my dissertation but didn't complete my doctorate – that rug got yanked out from beneath me by a dissertation committee who told me what to do, then decided in the final hours that no, it's not what they wanted. I'd been holding on by a thread to get it done. I had nothing left to give, including the money for another year of tuition. I was bereft and at a loss of what to do next. I chose to give away my furniture, let go of my house, and took myself and Lily out on the road in my truck.

I cried a lot. I missed my son. I'd taken myself on two unguided shamanic descents during my Master's and doctoral research, once with the Golden Gate Bridge, and then again with Fire. To say I wasn't grounded would be a hellish understatement.

Now here I am, after a far more hellish couple of years, which began last August with the intentional and unexplained disappearance of my son, my heart, and his continued absence from my life.

And I'm not a train wreck.

There's PTSD for sure. That's understandable. Lava and loss and ballistic missiles will do that.

Why is this time different? Why am I not a train wreck?

Probably because I didn't give up seven years ago when I was. I didn't get dead. I kept going. I made it. I'm no longer one person in public and another behind closed doors.

I chose to lean into that pain, not to waste it. It taught me to see pain as the gift that it is, because it breaks us open, it upsets our status quo. It releases the parts of us that went into hiding because they didn't fit with who others thought we were supposed to be.

What saved me now are the things I learned then. Perseverance. If there was something on the other side of that darkness, then there must also be something on the other side of this. The lava was horrific, the losses heartbreaking. But out of it came friendships, shifted perspectives, new priorities, and, bonus, less tolerance for the BS of the people who'd like to control me. Of those who'd like to feel superior. And who aren't. And know it.

I'm content. I'm okay. I'm a geeky Wander Woman and I chose love. I chose you. And I choose me.

Henry David Thoreau says the best we can hope for is to lead quiet lives of desperation.

He's wrong.

The best we can hope for is that we never give up. Even when we've lost all hope, we must kindle the memory of once having had hope. Then hold onto it. Hard. And keep going.

You never, ever have to settle.

Every decision
I've ever made has been an act of desperation
disguised as a leap of faith.

CHAPTER 42:
Ready

10/27/18

Last summer, I came down from the mountains in California to a heartbreak that opened me to wounds both ancient and new. I thought it was enough to want to die. I didn't.

The stars aligned and the universe conspired to find more ways to break me, with ballistic missiles, lava, lightning, and hurricanes. And loss. And our hearts broke. And then, again, and again. Then again. More times than we could count. Until the breakings, which were all openings, began to lose the memory of how to remain closed.

Too exhausted or overwhelmed from the daily deluge, I quit attempting to knit the pieces back into their heart-shaped container, at once larger, and yet not enough for the next breaking.

We are not meant, as the Chinese proverb says, to pour gold into the cracks to seal it up. We are not vases. We are human souls. We are meant to crack open so our light can shine through.

Our hearts are meant to be like a sieve, or a screen, so water and fire mostly pass through...and there are some breakings...those that run deep, that may linger. And hurt longer...and then they too are meant to move on.

Leaving bits of things behind. And we get to choose...to hold onto the things, the angers and fears and resentments, or to the memories of what we loved. We are kidding ourselves to think that there is ever joy without a touch of grief inside.

And I take little credit for any of this. I give that to the relentlessness of the year. The booming nighttime explosions, as Puna too, broke open. Nights and days that forced us to live in the moment. Minutes on top of each other, knowing there were no plans to be made because where you wanted to go was no longer there.

To live next to and on top of living, breathing lava, that exploded and crept and poured from inside of our planet running just beneath our feet. To watch it crawl and ooze and shift course and then consume. And create. To watch for months. And to feel the love of our community as the destruction brought us together and sustained us.

To have our hearts broken. Broken open. It's a terrible gift we are all given. It is our instinct for preservation to try to escape from such terrible pain. But we aren't meant to escape it. Not meant to spend our days and years trying to make it what it was, or in building an impenetrable wall around it. We're not meant to waste the pain by closing.

The pain is meant to break us open. And we are meant to stay that way.

Not in the pain.

But in the joy that holds the bits of grief.

I always thought surrendering meant giving something up.
Now I know it means allowing something in.

10/31/18

Live feed
https://www.youtube.com/watch?v=x5vK-oZTyJc&feature=youtu.be

Meet the Fun Times RV guys as they're loading the Miata.

CHAPTER 43:
Meltdown

11/2/18

Live feed
https://www.youtube.com/watch?v=n2dkso9FVAs&feature=youtu.be

...I am a little worse for wear. I had a nap today and I'm at some rest stop in New Mexico. I don't know how to turn my heater on and it's cold, so I'm going to bundle up. I have a pair of socks. I planned ahead...

...I left in the middle of the night to avoid traffic. I wasn't thinking that truck drivers are pretty smart people, and they don't want to drive in Phoenix and Tucson in the traffic either. So, there were a lot of trucks on the road. I tried to stop and get gas but when I pulled into a gas station and I looked at the pull-through pumps for RVs and cars I was like, with that trailer...I was too tired...

...I looked at where the trucks were driving through, and I was totally intimidated. So, I was like, forget about it. I've still got half a tank, drive on. That's how I got to where I am. I landed in Phoenix three weeks ago. It's like some kind of weird time warp...

...I look at these 45-foot buses that people drive and think, I could never. Then I start doing the math. My RV is 31 and 1/2 feet, add about two feet a hitch and about twelve feet of trailer. And guess what...

...One thing I'm noticing, is I never used to be reluctant to ask for help when I was on the road, but since leaving Hawaii I feel exposed and want to stay inside. I get anxious about being seen. Which goes back to the sensation of having left myself behind...

...Somebody thanked me for sharing my process, for doing this out loud. I believe in telling the scary parts because I don't believe in only showing you the parts where "Yay is me," and "Aren't I so amazing?" I'm not amazing. I'm totally clueless. I'm emotionally wrung out. On empty. I get scared. If it hadn't been for Gary and Larry and Joey and Duke, I would have come out on the road as clueless as I was the last time, seven years ago. In every new adventure, no matter how exciting it might seem, I have a learning curve. I have the scary part...

CHAPTER 44:
Truth or Consequences

11/3/18

Live feed
https://www.youtube.com/watch?v=AZyKCVP-SjU&feature=youtu.be

...I made it, I'm in Truth or Consequences...everything is set up...I'm going to sit in the geothermal baths...pictures later...

11/5/18

Live feed
https://www.youtube.com/watch?v=9BJdOGNCqRM&feature=youtu.be

...a quickie from the geothermal pool so you know what I'm talking about when I say I'm going for a soak...

11/5/18

There's been a barely conscious method to my madness. An urgency about getting things into place. Getting here, to Truth or Consequences. A place I came to for the first time, in my first RV, seven years ago this month.

At that time, it wasn't a plan. I came for a work trade in Williamsburg, a town that merges with Truth or Consequences. The work trade was at Desert Haven Animal Shelter and turned out to be a bust, so I moved into town, along with most of the rest of the workers. We moved to Artesian Springs RV and Bath House. Which is where I am now.

It was snowing.

They said it never snowed.

I pointed to my kayak buried beneath two feet of powder and said, "Well...."

The rest of that time includes busted furnaces, a stalker and a cut fuel line, going to Texas, breaking down on the bridge to Galveston, (finding out there's a bridge to Galveston), and engine failures, which all eventually led to my landing at Madre Grande Monastery, in Dulzura, California. Stories for another time.

Truth or Consequences was once known as Hot Springs, New Mexico. Then the game show, Truth or Consequences, offered a $10,000 prize for the first town that changed its name to theirs. Hot Springs won. I think they lost.

What I didn't know when I was here before is that the town sits atop the largest geothermal aquifer on the continent. The free-flowing water that runs through the bathhouses, and that we soak in, is 250,000 years old. I just thought it was another hot spring.

> *Maybe I'm a naïve, unicorn-riding tree hugger*
> *who got dosed with reality, and magic doesn't exist,*
> *and miracles don't happen, and everything I've ever*
> *thought was true was incorrect.*

I didn't think I'd ever return for more than a pass through to visit my friends who're still here.

But once I got to Phoenix, that Place that is more than a name, but also the mythological bird rising from the ashes, I knew it was where I needed to be. Where I had to be. I had to be here. I had to. I tried not to. But I was compelled. Drawn. Magnetized.

Things happened so fast. My car, my RV, both within days of my arrival.

Galvanized by moments of razor-sharp grief. Pushing it away for another day, and with the promise of soon.

Soon.

You were with me in my culture shock of traffic and people and getting lost. Driving through the night. Crying. Then driving some more. Finding my pace. White knuckling the steering wheel and reminding myself to breathe.

Finding my place. You were with me.

And this urgency. Through the physical pain and the pushing through. To have it all in place. Falling into place. This Place. My things in place.

Because of the promise to myself to write. And to you. To write. And my body knows. It's almost time. The writing time. The remembering. The integrating. The blessings and friendships and gratitude and grief and the love.

The seeking. The finding. Of friends and safe places and soft blankets and warm boots. The nibbling at my edges of the words as they begin to whisper. Gurgling up from my psyche as these ancient waters do, through river stones with imperceptible, persistent force. Soon they'll stop with their whispers and they will yell. They will consume. Me. To speak the words I can almost but not quite hear. To speak with impunity.

Through the Fire. The Earth. The Water. The Air. Finally, in a place dry enough to demold even my jungle saturated body.

Last time I was here, I felt I was in Consequences. I was in a different kind of pain. The train wreck kind. Now I am in Truth, and not a train wreck, even though I know it's going to hurt like one. Fire healing and Water burning.

CHAPTER 45:
Writing Elves

Hunter S. Thompson wasn't always a wild and crazy writer. When he finally gave up on writing right, and decided to go with a more uninhibited style, he said it was "like falling down an elevator shaft and landing in a pool full of mermaids."

I understand this. What I wrote yesterday sounds to me like I was saying when it's time to write, when the whispering becomes yelling, that it's out of control.

Quite the opposite.

It means that what's been brewing in the back of my head, the fragments of ideas and raw materials that my brain has gathered, are ready. It's this insistence that cannot be resisted. It's why so many of my articles, blogs, posts, essays, rants, blurts, whatever you call them, are written in the middle of the night. They wake me up. They beat on the inside of my skull until I wake up and tap them out on my phone. Because they're ready when they're ready, not when I am.

Until that moment my involvement is minimal. I'm just the conduit, the receiver of ideas.

At the risk of publicly proclaiming I'm cray cray (which most of you know anyway 🙉😊), I refer to this process as feeding the elves. My elves aren't benevolent, or ethereal, they are the trickster, they are the Menehune. They are Loki. They are Coyote, who came to me as a child, fully formed, biting me on my arm to wake me up. Letting me know that they were watching. My elves revel in taking ideas both sacred and sacrosanct, and running amuck with them. Unraveling them, combining them with each other, discarding what doesn't fit.

I believe it was they who fed me the questions that got me kicked out of Sunday school when I was four. They don't see the world in the way they're supposed to see it, they see it the way that it actually is.

In the fairy tale *The Elves and the Shoemaker*, the shoemaker lays out the makings of shoes each night in preparation for the morning, but each night the elves sneak in and complete the task by morning. The shoemaker doesn't know this, so he thinks it's magic until he discovers the truth.

I also used to think the way my ideas for writing appeared, essays and ideas fully formed, was magic. I didn't know that the elves are always there, listening for the material so they can create the ideas. They've got files and files and files, full of puzzle pieces I've gathered without knowing, which they fiddle with endlessly, until they've got a complete something. Which is when the skull tapping happens. It's ready, they say, as they hand me the story at my personal witching hour of 2 a.m.

Mystics call this channeling. Carl Jung calls this introverted intuition. Empaths call it getting a download. Hunter S. Thompson calls it falling into a pool of mermaids.

I call it intriguing. Exciting. Fun. Scary. Annoying, Fascinating. My gift. My superpower.

I used to be afraid of the process because I didn't always know what I was going to say until it was written. I was afraid you'd disagree with me, say that I'm wrong, and I was afraid I would get into trouble. That my ideas would be ridiculed. That it would hurt my heart.

I'd be lying if I said I'm not afraid anymore. Just not as afraid. I'm still careful about which ideas I share. The elves seem satisfied once it's written and usually don't concern themselves with whether anyone besides me reads it. I think they're playing the long game. They know that if I write it down, eventually I'll be compelled to talk about it. They are patient. Lulling me into a sense of safety, knowing that, if they wait long enough, and poke me with an idea long enough, in the end, I will take the risk.

One of the stories I was afraid to share was the first one I posted on Hawaii Tracker, on 7/17/18, to an audience of 45,000 readers.

I was afraid it wouldn't be received as I intended, that it might hurt or offend someone and cause them more grief. That you'd think I was whining or being dramatic. But you loved it. And in so doing, you opened the floodgates for the other stories and ideas that have been waiting on the shelves.

Pele, Aila'au, and the persistence of the elves, were only a few of the elevator shafts that landed me here in this wondrous pool of mermaids.

11/8/18

I'm not ready. Not yet.

I talk of elves and mermaids and then I say I'm not ready.

Because I'm not. Because they aren't. I can't tell a story I don't know yet. My insides are full of emptiness and silent surviving.

I rush myself to ease my anxiety. I spend time getting settled, keeping busy, sounding right, being sad, being fine, and doing things I'd never do, like scrubbing my carpet on my hands and knees. All pieces in the distraction caused by the sounds of silence pinging through me. What happened?

Honestly. Honestly. There's no way I'm okay. On the inside.

What we went through. What anyone who's gone through a traumatic event goes through. It leaks into your bones, burrows under your skin, pillages your psyche.

You don't see it, but you can taste it. You can feel it on your skin and in your hair. It's beneath your fingernails. It's stuck in the back of your throat, and in the pit of your stomach.

You don't know until you look in the mirror and don't recognize who's looking back. You don't know until something happens, something less traumatic, something unrelated.

You notice because your response surprises you. You snap. You take a joke personally. Your tolerance is less, you feel bone weary, breakable. Porcelain, not plexiglass.

There's an invisible line that says to mourn for 'x' amount of time is okay. To pass that line isn't okay. You will be judged. They will suggest to you that it's time to move on. Time to let go. Sometimes they're right. And sometimes they need to STFU and mind their own business.

Plus, survivor's guilt. Maybe you didn't suffer the same losses as your neighbor. Or your neighbor's recovery seems quicker than yours. Or you didn't lose anything but you're still grieving. Or maybe you secretly wish you'd lost everything, so you could begin again. You're not sure what you're supposed to be feeling. You aren't sure what you're feeling at all.

Your brain goes into overdrive trying to figure out how to grieve in a manner that is both timely and appropriate. You lash out. You lash in. You hide. You say you're fine, and maybe you even believe it. All while your brain turns the Rubik's Cube in an attempt to sort itself out in spite of your words.

The infinite ways the cube gets perpetually turned can manifest in envy and jealousy, depression, resentment, despair, guilt, and anger. Or denial. But denial is just a cover for the bullet-shaped judgments that start hitting the people around us. Hurting them because we're hurting and trying not to.

Because:

- I don't want to be like them. They're weak.
- I'm being like them so it must be okay.
- I wish I was like them.
- I'm right, they're wrong.
- They're right. I'm wrong.

But we can't judge other people's outsides by our insides.

There's no way out of the rat maze except to not go into it in the first place. If you find yourself there, it's best to jump out quickly.

The answers are elsewhere. They are in the mirror. Even when the eyes staring back feel like those of a stranger. It's in the acceptance that the feelings don't feel how we want them to. That to be 'fine' is to be Fucked up, Insecure, Neurotic, and Emotional. And it's actually FINE and human to be these things. In the moment. During the trauma. After the event. To have good days. Then sad ones.

To stay there is what I fear. To slip backwards into the belief that I AM those things instead of remembering I'm only feeling them. Only.

And so, I've been rushing toward the writing. And the nesting. And the processing. When it's just not time. We can give ourselves time.

I cannot produce a damn thing for a while without need for justification. Or labeling it 'wasting time.'

There is no one invisible grief/anger/mourning size fits all.

It's possible, and it's okay, to feel joy while you're still in pain. While you're still sad.

You're not over it. You'll never be over it, and the stories wanting to be told aren't going anywhere.

Because we don't have to DO, in order to heal. Sometimes we just need to sit. Or color. Or watch a lot of *Star Trek*. And *RuPaul*.

In order for the world to heal, your story needs to be heard.
When you're ready.

CHAPTER 46:
Temperature

11/14/18

I think I finally found my perfect temperature artesian bath – 102 degrees.

I also discovered a connection to Puna. During the eruptions in Hawaii, the temperature in the pools here in T or C went up an average of eight degrees. Some got so hot they had to be closed.

Suddenly, I don't feel so far from home.

Makes me wonder just how hot Ahalanui got before she was taken (both being geothermal).

Earlier today, I went looking for my next Lily and found a grey tabby kitten who was just a few months old. She looked so much like Lily that I couldn't not cry.

I said, "That's her."

And they said, "She's not ready yet."

Allegory received. I went home alone.

Before leaving, I did sit with the little kitty for a while, feeling how much I still hurt. I have days when I think this part is past, but then seeing a kitty who reminds me of Lily gets past my armor and I know the pain is still there. I can't believe how much it hurts.

I needed a break from feeling for a while, but today Lily spoke to me through this little feline simile, letting me know I'm not ready yet.

Afterwards I went to the baths to float in that perfect water thinking about the kitty who'll someday find me. When I'm ready.

11/21/18

I've got this kind of experiment going with myself. I'm unschooling my life.

Unschooling is one of the subsets in homeschooling, and it's one I practiced when I homeschooled my son in middle school.

It's kind of scary because the basic idea is that you don't follow a curriculum. You expose your child to ideas; you take them on field trips. Mostly though, you follow their lead.

We did a lot of cool things in my son's unschooling days. One of our favorite unschooling projects was the Fromage Soirée.

Sean loved cheese so we'd invite friends over and ask them to bring a few cheeses of their choice. We'd also buy an assortment of our own. Together he and I would research the history, geography, and proper serving and pairing of each cheese. Then he'd present each one to our guests.

While our Soirées were great fun, the area he really dove into was video games. That scared me. What could come out of that but a lot of isolation, and wasted time on the computer?

I was wrong. When he returned to public school, he had interests he wanted to pursue. He got involved in computer and video classes, leadership, and the drama club. He filmed the football games and ran the A/V for school plays. By the time he was 17 he'd won awards and was filming engagement parties. He even toured with a rock band in Florida, all because of his early interest in gaming.

He's fearless when it comes to exploring and taking risks.

Some of this is likely in his nature. He was born this way. But at least part of this is because I refrained from 'shoulding' him. He learned to trust himself and the universe.

This is my experiment with me now. I'm breaking the habit of 'shoulding.' Like, I should get up and get things done. Or, I should write, or I should do my laundry (I really should). Or I should respond to people I don't want to respond to, so they don't feel bad.

It's a hard habit to break. We are 'should'd' all of our lives. We should say please and thank you. We should go to school. We should remain silent and not air our dirty laundry. We should carry our burdens and pain in silence. We should forgive. Let go. Move on. Be positive.

How do we know who we are, or how we feel, when at every turn there's already a 'should' there waiting for us, telling us how to be? How can we know who we are if we don't take the time to really know what WE want, instead of adhering to a cultural norm past its expiration date?

It's unlikely you'll discover your true self on the inside of a norm.

There's a massive hoard of life and business coaches, and books and workshops, all with the intent of helping you discover your true purpose.

I would argue that we already know what that is, and it's hidden in plain sight beneath a pile of unexamined 'shoulds'.

Which is why I'm unschooling my life.

I'm in the great unraveling. And I can't knit a new sweater until that's done.

So far this looks like sleeping in, listening to music, learning to use my MacBook, and watching *Downton Abbey*.

I know that it won't always be this way. That when the time comes, I'll begin again.

Because nature truly does abhor a vacuum.

In order to be your true self, you have to let go of who you think you are.

CHAPTER 47:
Tears

1/2/19

I just stood in front of my full-length mirror and cried. Not for long, and not for the reasons you might think.

I've been reading books on epigenetics, emotional DNA (an idea I've been drawn to for over 20 years). Epigenetics is the understanding of how unresolved trauma, behavior patterns, and even our perspectives are transmitted between generations, as well as between each of us, by secondary means. By a kind of osmosis. Nearness to each other's energy fields.

I love this stuff. It's an exciting time of discoveries in neuroscience and psychology. However, it's not new to traditional and indigenous cultures, just to us, and our Western mindset's insistence that logic be tangible. Science is playing a game of catch-up with what ancient cultures have understood for millennia.

Why does this matter? It matters because we're missing the clues to the answers we don't always know we're looking for.

Too often we don't know what we're asking. We're ricocheting through our lives, pinging from the manic to the depressive, the joy to the grief. The ups to the downs. I've had my fair share of the ups. Grand adventures, great friends, incredible experiences. If you flip that book over there's been an equal amount of pain and distress and grief and loss.

In each instance, the emotions I've chosen to respond with I thought were mine alone. But they aren't. They are the gifts passed down through I've no idea how many generations of ancestors. Their unresolved trauma. Their response to love. Their response to betrayal.

These are unconscious gifts that stop here. Which is a tall order. How do I stop something that I've thought all along was me, acting alone, upon my thoughts? Is this the deeper meaning to Socrates saying that an unexamined life isn't worth living?

I thought I was done. That I'd gone far enough. But there is still damage around me, in the words and faces of people that I love. And as we are all each other's ancestors, my best thing to do is continue the work. By helping to stop the transmissions between generations, from one to another, from me or through me, and to do it now.

So why did I cry in the mirror?

I cried because I saw an almost 55-year-old woman, standing alone, with a mess of hair and imperfect skin. I saw her Eeyore pajamas, and her peacock-patterned fleece robe. I saw the incongruity of her violet tank top with her hand-knit red slippers. I saw no makeup.

I saw beauty.

Me, looking into my own eyes and seeing exquisiteness and pain and progress and acceptance.

And I loved me for it. I loved that I didn't quit the healing or the processing; even when I was told enough is enough. Or better yet, to just medicate. I loved who I was looking at, really looking at, without reservation.

I love how I've shifted from the self-loathing I lived with well into my twenties and thirties. I wondered at the pain and then sat down to get back to work.

That pain I've always carried isn't mine alone.

It's about them and us and you and me. My mission in this life is to continue to be part of transcending those transmissions. What we do for ourselves, we do for each other. When we heal, others heal with us. This is more than words, this is epigenetics. This is energy. This is quantum. This is real.

The truth is subjective and irrelevant.
What you believe is what defines your reality.
The truth has very little to do with it.

CHAPTER 48:
Missing

1/14/19

This idea. It's got no structure, no form. It's grief and wanting what's next. It's the guilt of letting go.

It's about missing my friends. It's about missing the life that was. It's about being too tired to start again. It's about my heart being in too many places, and in too many pieces. It's about accepting that it's time for something different. It's about the longing from my gypsy soul.

I wanted Puna to be my forever place. I thought I could make myself stay. I followed a trail of sparkly breadcrumbs to my jungle and fell in love with its mysterious, chaotic soul.

I don't want to go back. I don't want to see. I want to freeze the before of it. When it was the charm of my wagon and the nights of warm rain, asleep in the loft, snuggled up with my sweet Lily, and my visions for the future.

It's the Warm Pond. It's camping at Pohoiki. It's the peacefulness of my road. It's the quiet ache of abandoning a dream and my desire, because it's gone anyway.

It's about letting go of who I tried to be so I can return to the being of me.

I want the before when I believed that what I imagined could be real.

I never want to leave. I just don't want to go back.

1/18/19

So. I'm going home tomorrow and have been feeling all the emotions.

Joy! I get to see my people!

And grief. For all the obvious reasons.

What will I encounter that is new? How will it feel to go to Pohoiki? To see my land. To touch the lava.

Rain or shine, this is where I spent my time. Where Lily lounged on the rocks or reconnoitered beneath the palms. Where she would come out of our jungle, daintily picking her way through the mud, to greet me in the street when I came home.

This is where I swam and attended potlucks. Played cribbage. Chanted in women's circle. Had moonlight swims. And where I did so much healing. Made forever friends.

Others say the same thing, that losing Ahalanui was the hardest day. It didn't just happen in a day though. It took months. It happened over weeks and days. The flow was headed that way. Then it stopped and Puna heaved a sigh of relief. Then it began again, and from another direction. And it kept coming. We felt the awful ache as it inched closer. Eating the land like it was chewing our flesh.

We watched. Hoping. It no longer felt like it was blood pumping through our hearts, but salty tears, too fat to fit in the veins they weren't meant for. It was sluggish, we were involved reluctantly, and involuntarily. We had no choice. There was nothing we could do. If the pumping stopped, our hearts would stop, which would bring us ease but also death.

Then we woke up and it was gone.

There's a hole in me where it still lives, and where we still swim.

CHAPTER 49:
Coming Home

1/20/19

Swept with grief. Terrible timing. Halfway across the Pacific Ocean on my way home. To Hawaii. Olivia Newton John's *Xanadu* on the headphones. When you've practiced being strong, it takes something ridiculous to crack through your veneer. *Xanadu* will do.

It's not just the lava that hurts. Or Lily. It's not just the pond. Or my treasures.

It's not just my wagon. Or everything I went through with my son, or all the relatives who couldn't care enough to pick up the phone and say, "I hope you're okay. I know things aren't great with us. But I care." And it's not about the few who did.

It's all of it. And it's how bloody freaking much I struggled.

It's the mud and rain and cockroaches and rats and coquis and slugs. It's about enormous albesia, and giant ohia trees falling in the night. Its black pigs grunting in the dark. It's the damn red ants staging a coup on my face. It's the beauty and wonder and awe of living alone in the rainforest of Hawaii. It's about every shade of green.

It's the falling asleep to the rain. It's the waking up to the 'bueno' birds at sunrise. It's the jumping out of bed to feed Lily, then getting into the Miata to rush to Lava Tree Park to use the bathroom.

It's the weeds that grew two feet in two days. It's discovering a tree growing out of my chair. It's my magical outdoor shower. It's my quiet street where Lily was queen. It's hot tea neighbor. It's my health halting me in my tracks, forcing me to choose between giving up, or learning things I never would have had I been able to move at full speed.

It's the few days when the dream came to life with others. It's about how many people came to my land, and then went. It's about no one making it more than three nights. My land didn't want them. Their fear got the most of them. They saw things that frightened them. They left. It's my seeing things that helped me want to stay.

It's the machetes, and the sweat rolling into my eyes. It's the hand-clearing and learning the face of my land like you would that of a beloved. It's the Transfer-Station treasures, and the kindness of strangers. It's the regrouping. It's the accepting that until my land said yes to someone else being there, I was on my own. It's the surrendering.

It's the coming up with a new plan. Over and over. And over. It's the reconciliations and the long overdue goodbyes. It's about feeling useless, and it's about coming back to life. It's about finding my reason why.

It's about bliss and despair. Hope and grief. It's about being perfectly happy for no good reason. And it's about a thousand moments of WTF was I thinking.

It's the dreams. The dreams of a lifetime. Dreams, whose degree of difficulty were beyond my scope. It was having no clue how hard breathing life into them was going to be. It's the crushing disappointments, screaming out to Pele, or whoever was listening, why did you bring me here if this is how it's going to be? It's the feelings of betrayal.

What do you want from me?

To be. It's the Being.

It's the friends. Here and there. It's the shattering, and the scattering, of us, and it's the beveled pieces we carry of each other when we go. It's this Puna ohana, and by extension, everyone who came with us through the stories and pictures we shared that went around the world. It's the strength and camaraderie and tremendously endless love. It's the ways in which we recognize each other in strangers.

It's the magnitude of the gifts received in ridiculous packaging. It's the many lives worth of understanding and insight and true wisdom I've encountered in four years that feel more like 20. Or 2,000. It's getting that this is what the theory of relativity means.

That time is relative. That we can learn nothing, do nothing, for four years. Or we can take a chance and end up learning it all.

It's the commitment to the commitment. It's the irony of making the commitment, to one place, to giving up my Wander Woman ways, and then being gifted a gypsy wagon within days of moving onto my land. It's ignoring that synchronicity and calling it a 'coincidence.' Even though I know better. It didn't mean I wasn't supposed to be there. It meant it was one more step along the way. If I hadn't ignored that would any of this have been any easier?

I don't believe in signs. Synchronicity isn't a superstitious sign, it's an energetic confirmation. Energy in alignment manifests the next right thing. It's finding out that it was THE gypsy wagon. The only one on the island. The one with a history. The one that escaped Kilauea in the eighties, only to be caught and consumed by her almost 40 years later.

There is a difference between synchronicity, and superstition. Synchronicity was me posting a pic of a ginormous black pig, buying land months later, then finding out that pig had been trapped on my land.

Superstition is cutting your leg on tin roofing and being told it's a 'sign'. Of what?

Carelessness. That's what.

*The biggest wild black pig I've ever seen and it once lived
on my land!*

It's the feeling that after more than three decades of coming and going, of always believing Hawaii would someday be my 'for the rest of my life home,' that it's not. I can feel this book closing. It's about the contradictions and the setbacks and the triumphs.

It's about finding the form in my own chaos.

Because I want to wander more than I want the Place that owns me and holds my heart.

It's the big goodbye. Because I don't belong there. I belong everywhere.

Which I've always known. And never accepted. And none of it is forever

Oh god. We've landed and I am home.

1/22/19

Live feed
https://www.youtube.com/watch?v=ErXv4MtVGBI&feature=youtu.be

Driving up Pohoiki to dead end of lava

Live feed
https://www.youtube.com/watch?v=xOXL20CtVII&feature=youtu.be

New black sand beach at Pohoiki

CHAPTER 50:
Anger

1/23/19

I'm sick. And I'm angry. Angry that I'm sick and wondering if it's my normal sick, or if it's allergies to the doggie dander, or the jungle fungal.

I've been here four days and I've been out of bed for only one of them. Granted, it was a great day.

The universe has this way of taunting me when I make definitive statements, like, I belong here. And yes, I'm taking this to an unreasonably personal level.

Because I'm angry. Enraged. That solid, I want to punch something kind of fury. Except I'm not a puncher. And. I'm fucking pissed. At the lava.

Then I stand and look at it and I feel blank. Because there's absolutely nothing I can do about it. I want my life back.

And it's good that I'm so angry. Again. Some people go their entire lives never being angry about the justifiably angry situations that happen. We are taught to skip the anger stage of grief. It's not healthy to be angry.

Bullshit. What's not healthy is stifling anger to the point of depression or sickness. Anger internalized becomes depression, or passive aggression. Or outright physical aggression.

Anger is an emotion, not an action. Expressing anger doesn't do a damn thing to cause us harm. Repressing it does. Depression and aggression do. Anger can inspire passion to act, to make a change. It can motivate. It gets us moving when nothing else will. Anger makes me think.

But anger scares most people. They think aggression is anger. They fear their own anger, so they want to avoid yours.

And yet here I am being angry. Really pissed off. I'd gotten my life to a place where I was managing my health concerns and elevating my quality of living. I had next step plans and the means to carry them out. Life was about to get a whole lot easier before the damn rug got pulled from beneath me.

I'm not being reasonable. I get that. I don't care. I'm not being zen. I'm not zen. I'm a fallible human being who is having a huge pity party in her own honor. I'm pissed.

I want to punch the lava. I want to see it crumble. I want to be back in my van camping at Pohoiki, Lily snuggled up next to me while we fall asleep to the moon rising and the surf pounding. I want to see Lily lounging beneath the coconut palms at the pond.

I want to be talking to my mango trees and watching my heliconia grow. I want to see the freesia tree in bloom and the wild orchids in the ferns. I want to see the ohia bloom. I want to look out my loft window into the crater, and over the edge of the cliff into the cave. I want to see the parts of my land I hadn't cleared yet, and hadn't met, and now never will.

I want to do a lot of things I'll never get to do again. And I'm really, really, really, angry about that.

Some might be offended by my anger. Might ask, "Who are you to question the will of Pele? Or to think you are immune? We've lost too, to fires and floods and hurricanes and wars."

I'm not questioning anyone's will, be they human or deity.

Nor do I think I'm alone.

What I'm doing is I'm being pissed on my own behalf. I'm being unreasonable because I'm tired of the silver lining. I'm tired of skipping the anger part because of what someone might think. Or because I'm not being reasonable and fair.

Yes. The lava is magnificent. Living through an event such as this was life-altering in every way. I feel strangely lucky to have been here for it. It will always be one of the most awe-inspiring events of my life.

But bloody hell already.

What I want now is some chicken soup, and I want a big, burly man with massive forearms to wrap himself around me and tell me we're going to work this all out, so go back to sleep.

And he won't forget to say, "It'll be okay, Punkin'."

Gonna go watch RuPaul now. It soothes the savage beast in me.

1/26/19

I'm not a child stomping her foot in the mud and shaking her curls at the lava. I'm just drawn that way.

Is it a problem that I believe in miracles and magic and fairy dust? Or is it my reliance upon them that creates the challenge?

I can't point at a thing outside of myself and say, definitively, that is what my rage was about. I could name a hundred things, some I could have done something about, some were out of my hands. It doesn't matter. The details aren't the answer. The point isn't in the minutiae.

But there is an answer.

I came across the perfect book within minutes of my pissed off post. Literally. I pressed send, got out of the van, walked into the office and there it sat on a desk.

Anger, by Thich Nhat Hahn.

I'm not finished reading it, and I have a list of ideas for further exploration, but I had the answer to my rage within the first few pages.

It's me I'm angry with. Fairly or unfairly, it's me.

I made some decisions. My life in the jungle was far from easy. My body couldn't do what needed doing. I was still making it happen but why so stubborn?

Because some of it was a dream inside the dream. It was being in love with the dream. It was the magic in the moments. Falling asleep in the loft of the gypsy wagon with the jungle folding around me. It was camping in the van and moonrises at Pohoiki. It was sunrise and the napping honu at Magic Sands in Kona. It was spooning with Lily while the rain pounded down outside. It was playing at the role of being a beach bum, even if I'm old enough to know better.

I will always have the sensations of these memories. Even when I forget, my body will remember. Memories of my relationship to the land, the aina. Ecopsychology. They're part of my makeup now. Emotional DNA. Epigenetics.

And I was treading water. Waiting for what was next. But the next that I was anticipating never came. This is the next that did.

I'm angry that I did exactly as I pleased. I'm angry at myself for living in the moment and having those experiences I'd have otherwise gone on reading about someone else having and wishing it could have been me. I'm angry for remembering the good parts and paying less attention to the bad. For missing out on an imagined future, rather than loving the moments that are now.

I'm angry at myself for it not ending well.

Yet this is who I am. I'm curious. I want to know what's around the next corner, and I want to know it in person. It's ridiculous to be angry when I know for a fact that I'm going to continue doing it, and that if I had it to do over again, I would.

Life is made up of thousands of little dreams, strung together between the things that could have happened, and the things that did happen while wandering along the road less traveled. Life is about what we decided to do with the things we found along the way.

We've got to pay attention, or we'll miss them.

Thich Nhat Hahn says anger is part of us. And for us to not live in duality as if it is separate, and something we must rid ourselves of. Anger can be transformed with mindfulness. But we need anger. It is our compost for future endeavors.

Capitalize on your mistakes, for every stumble, fall,
or misstep is part of your sacred dance.

2/8/19

I refuse, absofuckinglutely refuse, to allow myself to be taken out again.

I'm going back to living my life outfucking loud, playing by my own rules, and writing books about it, as I please. Don't worry. The books aren't about you. Unless they are. And if you didn't want me to write about it, then you shouldn't have done it.

I'm not giving one tiny fuck about what anyone thinks about me. People can believe terrible lies about me, without consideration, and I know that no amount of trying to measure up changes a goddamn thing. So, if you are going to talk, and judge, then by all means, let me give you something to talk about... I am sick and fucking tired of my people making shit up about me. It just goes on and on and fucking on, now by people who are jacked up on drugs, or their own fear, who are telling more fucking lies about me, to more people who are too stupid to look for the truth.

No more. People will treat me right or get out.

I've spent my life, up to now, going back. Out of love, or fear, I let myself be soft. Fuck soft. It hurts. I'm tired of hurt. I love fiercely, loyally, and out loud. I'm going to get that back from those who truly love me and want me in their lives. Because I'm worth it. I finally get that I'm not second class, or a bad seed, a slut, a liar, a thief, or crazy, nor am I doomed. I do not march to the beat of the wrong drummer. Nor am I paranoid. I'm a good person. I'm a damn good woman. 🕯

All summed up in one look. And my use of the word fuck need not be construed as anger. It's emphasis.

CHAPTER 51:
Energies

2/20 and 2/20a

Live feed
https://www.youtube.com/watch?v=nLOG-uMCgVY&feature=youtu.be
https://www.youtube.com/watch?v=Wr-zGgcxubM&feature=youtu.be

Driving through Leilani – little or no words

2/20/19

Fissure 8 is now creating its own lightning storms.
Today was insane. A whirling eddy of chaos over Pahoa. Vog thick as pea soup.

So. Wow. Just wow.

The way I'm so overwhelmed by the swirl of emotions and the vortex of energies that the eruptions here have released. Eruptions that have released lava, along with the magma, the energies from the eighties, the fifties, the 1800s, and from times the scientists haven't yet identified.

Those energies, trapped in the lava from those past times, they have no place here, yet here they are. We are encountering them as they look for where they belong, and we are responding to their chaos without knowing that they exist.

The written words don't come easily or spontaneously as I'm accustomed to them doing.

What is this place that Puna has become? We're like a tube of toothpaste that's been squeezed into half of the container that once held us.

There are people who are okay. And people who say they are okay. And people who feel guilty for their homes being okay. And people who aren't here anymore. And people who are new. And people who are buying land in Leilani, a place once deeply forested, in order to turn it into paid parking lots for tourists to climb on. Forgetting this lava covers where someone's home was a short time ago. We're not a bloody theme park. We are not open for consumption.

And there are people who feel lucky to have been here for this experience, who are also incredibly sad over all we have lost. Like me.

I left for a few months. I watched from my RV in New Mexico as roads opened up in Puna, and people went home. Then I returned with the hope of getting in to see my property, to see with my own eyes where the lava has created ends of the roads that used to go all the way.

I'm not okay. I am sometimes okay. I thought I'd write so much while I was here. But the words are a dull roar in my skull.

It feels like we're not supposed to talk about the sadness anymore. It makes people uncomfortable.

Imago and I went to see John Stallman and Harry Durgin's slide presentation of the lava at the Palace Theater in Hilo. I laughed. I was in awe. I sat in the darkened theater and I cried. My eyes see what's there and what's gone all at once.

Life goes on. It's gone on. It's taken some along with it. Others grieve silently behind closed doors because we live in a world that's shortened the allotted time of grieving from a year, to a few months, to two weeks, to never.

That doesn't mean the grieving agrees. It means that it must transform itself into something else, like anger, or frustration, or a general numbing. Or illness. Or depression, or PTSD. Or the inability to handle the little things of life that once upon a time wouldn't have fazed, yet, they do now. Whatever its mask, it's still grief. Saying it isn't so doesn't make it not so.

So, I laugh when I encounter humor, and I cry when I have no other choice. And I mostly do it alone. Because I'm supposed to be okay.

3/1/19

What a trip. Memories in Maui. San Diego. Guam. Shaking my head at all the places I've lived, the people I've known, the people I've been. Feeling 55 and thinking I'm near the end, when really, I'm more likely at the beginning of another lifetime of adventures. And of people I will become.

Pahoa. Lahaina. Makawao. Pacific Beach. Leucadia. Encinitas. La Jolla. Truth or Consequences. Convents and monasteries, and Club Med. Gypsy wagons and boats And RVs. Each word another storyline. What I learned. The dangers and risks and the lucky moments of risky encounters with melting sex wax, mafia boyfriends and machine guns, water skiing, sailing, SCUBA, and kayaking. Flying fish and breaching whales. Dolphins riding in our wake. Piña Coladas and Long Island Iced Teas. Bonfires and *Bill Graham Presents*. Beachcombing by moonlight.

Hurricanes, floods, typhoons, and eruptions.

Three and a half decades of memories and treasure gathering. My sacrifices on the altar of Pele.

I've often thought how great it would be to have had someone alongside me who's shared in these memories. Someone to reminisce with.

Our relationship stronger and wiser for what we've shared with each other. But I'm realizing that I've shared them with myself. It doesn't take another person to be stronger and wiser. It takes paying attention and becoming awake. My relationship with me rocks. Especially considering how much I once disliked myself. And of where I once came from.

And before you jump on the advice-giving bandwagon, look in the mirror. Whatever you're about to say to me, it's for you.

I'd still love to find someone to share some adventures with, someone to lean on in the middle of the night when I get scared. But it's good to know that I've been with me all along, and that I've had my back every step of the way. I've shared my life with me.

I know for a fact that life can sucker punch me to my knees and I'll get back the fuck up and march on.

Or fly. Or ride. Or sail. Or whatever.

CHAPTER 52:
Anniversary

4/16/19

As we approach the one-year anniversary of the eruptions, Facebook is reminding me of the challenges and joys of the years on my land.

By this time last year, I'd made some peace with my jungle. My mud. My bugs, my weeds, and my varmints.

I had a plan. A reasonable one. One that wasn't pie in the sky, which, I admit, it had kinda been until that point. Not intentionally, but because I didn't know any better. And because I don't listen when I'm told that something I want to do can't be done.

I had my reasonable little routine. And my radius between the Pond and Pahoa, with my quiet little street in Lanipuna Gardens in between. I was hunkered down. Drinking Guinness in the moonlight and chasing cane toads with my phone.

Pele had other ideas. But in the moments of those days preceding the eruptions, my life felt idyllic. Hot tea neighbor dancing to Peter Gabriel in the rain. Spooning with Lily while the moon rose over the surf at Pohoiki. Potlucks with friends and finding heart-shaped corals in the pond. Driveways and blueprints for what was to come. Lily's squeaky purr...the one that said, I'm so glad you're here. I love you.

All tinged by twilight. Reminding me of when I was a kid outside playing, the sun almost down, the day almost done, and me eking out every last second on my bike as the wind flowed through my hair like freedom.

4/13/19

I was tired tonight and so ready to sleep. I got an earthquake alert earlier and was relieved to be here in the desert instead of home in Puna. I thought I wasn't bothered by it.

A few of the heart corals and a tiny opihi shell on prune fingers after many hours in the pond.

Then I closed my eyes and here I still am, hours later, wide awake.

We're coming up on one year. The 60,000 plus quakes we experienced during the months of eruptions and hurricanes are still residing in my body.

In bits and pieces. The snags that things get caught on.

For instance. I saw a comment on a Facebook post that said (and I'm paraphrasing), while it was devastating last year, it happened in a low population area with little infrastructure impacted, and how much worse it would be if eruptions happened on the Kona side.

As if.

When I questioned this, I was told it was because of the airport and freight planes, impacting food supply. Umm. Because we don't have an international airport, or a major shipping port in Hilo?

Oh, but wait. We do. It's like Puna is the proverbial red-headed stepchild.

Even if what they said is factually true, which I'm not saying, the reality is, thousands of people lost homes and jobs and animals and farms. Tourism tanked. Papaya and many other local crops that supply the islands were devastated.

There is no 'it would have been worse' case scenario for those of us who lost to the lava. We can't compare, we won't, any more than we would compare our lava to Nebraska's flooding, California's fires, or Katrina's winds.

I think only from the outside would anyone attempt to compare the apples to the oranges. Like some weird, pseudo-intellectual debate.

Me? I've still got the anxiety and my intellect can't talk me out of it. Not yet.

All the roadblocks you perceive are self-created.
So are they self-dissolved.
Unless lava is involved.
Then you're SOL.

CHAPTER 53:
Writing It Down

4/16/19

I'm in research mode for my lava book. This means I'm doing a lot of scrolling and gathering. Through Facebook videos, posts, pictures, and your comments. Through the articles I wrote and shared, and others that I wrote and tucked away.

I didn't mean to read the one about Lily tonight. I think I meant to never read it.

I haven't gotten to the stage where I totally immerse myself in these things, reading with a fine-tooth comb. I'm not ready for how much it hurt. Or to see my own rawness as it happened.

In the skimming through, my vision blurs with tears when one of your comments catches my eye. And my heart hurts, I think the way it hurt that whole time, like it's too big to fit inside my chest so must expand into my throat.

When it was happening, it felt like we were only ever in the moment. There was no living before or planning for after. There were so many moments, each day bringing another loss, each one enough to process for a lifetime, except we couldn't stop to ponder because we were already onto the next one.

We skipped like stones from Civil Defense alerts, to posts on Hawaii Tracker. We watched Ikaika, and Philip, and John, as they kept us informed from the Hub. We tuned in to Mick and Bruce who shared their views from the air. We went from earthquakes, to eruptions, to lava rivers, to hurricanes, to flash floods, and warnings from Civil Defense to "Don't Drown" in the flash floods. We were trying to keep up, trying to live as if what was happening wasn't more than we could handle, and living inside of the new normal as if it wasn't.

Writing is part of my healing. Writing makes things right. Part of my continuing evolution as I learn to live within the tension of opposites, where I'm both okay and broken-hearted.

I get that there's a cultural moratorium on grieving. That it's politically incorrect to be in pursuit of anything other than happiness. But I ascribe deeply to the idea that only an examined life is worth living, more so than I do to living a half-life that's fixated on positivity.

There is joy inside of the grief. Joy that can't be found elsewhere because it's tucked inside the dark places where we tell ourselves not to go.

Like the joy of my love for Lily.

CHAPTER 54:
Grief

*Remember last year when it rained (hard) for four months,
there was a ballistic missile crisis, and we had 12 minutes
to find shelter, then I sliced my leg open on tin roofing, then
the sun came out for two weeks, and then the floor was lava?*

Me either.

I know I lived through this. We lived through this. But really. It's hard to believe. And I forget. I still own an acre of land in Hawaii. It's just that it's covered in lava now instead of my glorious rainforest jungle.

And. We can't go home because there are no roads. And the Pond is gone.

Why (you ask, I ask, we ask) do we relive it when it would be better, less painful, to just move on, to forget about it? And how can we relive it at the same time we are resisting it because to look at it again so soon feels like interference with the rebuilding of our lives?

And we must be in both places because the healing is real. As is the pain.

I'm torn. I want to be over it. I want to be able to say, and to mean, that last year's months of endless eruptions and earthquakes and hurricane rains are something that happened but now I'm good.

I can't.

Not yet.

I've heard others say that they are, and maybe it's true. But maybe it's not. I'm okay a lot of the time. And then I'm not. Instead I'm grieving, like so many others, behind closed doors out of the misplaced belief that we're supposed to be over it. That to give in to grief heightens our suffering. That we must let go and move on. It was just a place, they were just things, everything ends. Accept the inevitable.

That's an ideal. An idea. A way of being that is something to work toward. An understanding of our human being-ness. Denying it hurts doesn't make it true. Those are just words. Words that will bury the wound in the fleshy recesses of judge and jury.

Spiritual ideals aren't meant to be weapons. They are meant to inspire us and to give us hope. And we forget. Grieving is an absolute act of courage and strength.

Because here's the thing.

There was too much to process at the time, last year, when it was all happening on top of itself. Each day brought enough for a lifetime. Yet, each morning, after a night of explosions and the jet-engine roar of fountaining lava, we were greeted by more. More loss. More fissures. More of more.

The reality is, facing our mortality with the ballistic missile crisis on January 13th was more than enough for anyone to deal with in one year. But that hour of impending threat, of not knowing, got buried beneath what came for us next.

Each day, we pushed yesterday's stories of earthquakes, flash-flood warnings, torrential downpours from impending hurricanes, crater collapses, road collapses, and land cracks, lava bombs and rushing lava rivers aside. Our self-defense from the onslaught lay in our ability to force each next thing down into our psyche. This is how the grief and loss and disbelief of weeks and months of yesterdays took up residence in our bodies in order to make room for what was happening in each next new today.

And now, those moments who took refuge in our flesh are saying, look at me. Look at me. LOOK AT ME. I am your heartache. I am your anxiety. And your sorrow. I am your trauma. There are too many of us for there to be enough room to remain in the darkness forever.

And we know that to heal we must go through it rather than get over it. So, we shed hot and heavy tears for the epic beauty and horror that it was.

Revisiting isn't about re-wounding, or being in a rut, or about being spellbound. It's not about pity or drama. It's about unearthing, because without this unspeakably courageous act we could remain stuck forever. Living out our lives governed by the memories left in our bones and in our blood.

We will grieve forever. In the moments. We all will. We will also go on.

None of us is so beyond being human, that of the death by a thousand pinpricks that it was, we won't forever not feel at least one of them.

Lava doesn't do what fires, floods, or hurricanes do. Lava takes away the bones. It melts and reshapes and burns and creates. It fills bays and builds mountains. It takes away the familiar face of the one we loved.

The one-year marker is a time for us to experience what happened from a distance of time and space, and to not do it alone. It's also our time to celebrate the ways in which we survived. Because it took courage and resilience and fortitude. Which is the definition of living in Puna on a good day. And we did it with class and with grace, on the not so good days.

Not every catastrophe offers the opportunity to heal as a community. Not every community is Puna Strong.

As this book is being completed, Hurricane Dorian has just devastated the Grand Bahamas. As I watch, I see how what we experienced in slow motion, over excruciating months, is what they experienced in a span of a few devastating days. I see the similarities as the community unites in their desire to rebuild, while at the same time so many must leave because there's nowhere left to live. They've lost the bones of their land too, not from a lava river, but from an ocean that rose out of its bounds and took over the island, gushing through homes and carrying away lives. Which brings me back to epigenetics. How much trauma has been left in its wake that will be passed on to others? How much of how we respond to trauma now has to do with how one of our ancestors dealt with another trauma before we were born?

5/3/19

Today we're sharing the photos and videos of a year ago when the first eruptions began, and they are unbelievable to see. This photo is the morning of, when I woke up thinking the jungle was on fire. I'd never seen a sky like this.

How did we not know that this unusual morning sky meant that soon more than the sky would be on fire?

I try to understand why my pain is so deep. I self-judge, telling myself I don't have the right to love so hard because I was only in Puna for four years.

Except that time is relative and my time in Puna feels like more than years, it feels like lifetimes. I'm not who I was when I got here.

Puna is a lifestyle you are required to give yourself over to. It calls for a complete immersion, a total mind, body, and soul commitment; because it's like living in no other place. And maybe that's why what happened, happened. The world needs what we had and without this you'd never have known we existed.

Puna is not the resort Hawaii you see in movies. It's rugged. It doesn't offer the kinds of distractions that you expect from a first-world location. Or from a holiday resort. Instead it confronts you, holding the mirror of your soul up to the tip of your nose.

You learn that living off-grid means you must shift how you perceive the world, and yourself, and what's necessary, and what you thought you needed. Even if you only see your neighbors' wave as they go by, you know that you're still in this unique situation, alone, together.

You're on the slopes of an active, living volcano. You know that you're here at the will of Pele, that your invitation could be revoked at any time, and you hope it never will be.

The outside world has to start making less sense in order to come to terms with the one you're now in.

Puna is where my decades of dreaming led me. It's the ONLY place, in the dozens of places I've lived, from Florida to Guam, that my Wander Woman soul has ever made a forever commitment to. The irony of this is that shortly after receiving Title, I was gifted the gypsy wagon that I called home.

Pele and the jungle and the aina and the elements took their toll on me. The land tested me. At first, things fell easily into place. Eventually that tapered off into the real challenges of living off-grid, alone with my cat, and for a while my puppy, in a tropical rainforest, full of mud and bugs and falling trees and hurricane threats. And mold that made me sick.

So many times, I would cry into my jungle, what do you want from me??? And over and over I would listen and learn and surrender and recommit. I went through the heat of many fires long before the lava came, each one teaching me something about priorities, and clarity, and about what matters. In this I'm not unique. Everyone is tested.

I've lived in Hawaii many times, over many years, and still, I was so very naive. I thought I was in partnership with the aina, and I thought I knew what that meant. I didn't.

It wasn't about being a good person or a spiritual one. The will and designs of the archetypal energies of a goddess, whether Pele or Gaia, or a god like Aila'Au, or an Element of Earth, Wind, Water, Fire, Wood, or

Meta,l are beyond the comprehension of the human brain. We can attempt to hazard a guess but it's presumptuous to think we could ever know.

Because I'd been through so many rites of passage on my land, I thought I had earned the right to be there, and to be protected. That somehow because I didn't run away during any of the hard times, something would keep my place safe now. Many of my friends believed the same thing. But she took it from me anyway. And even that is a presumption because it's not about me.

And that's what I mean about my human brain being unable to comprehend the inner workings of anything other than another human brain. We serve different purposes.

So, while I want to be okay, I've cried hard today. I feel I've failed to honor my commitment to the land because I chose to hele on, to leave Puna. My place is gone.

The Pond is gone. I'm not well enough yet to begin again. Lava took it all. Our homes, our neighborhoods, and our gathering places. We didn't lose our lives, but we did lose the lives we were living.

I sunk my heart and soul and being into my land. Over and over.

That's why it hurts so much.

I wasn't just visiting. I was home.

CHAPTER 55:
Okay

5/26/19

I love my post from one year ago today.

5/26/18

> *I was told tonight that the flow has NOT reached my place yet. How this is possible I'm not even going to question. Believing in the magic of the gypsy wagon for one more night. May the lava divert itself left again, and into those 500-foot craters behind my place.*

The emotional rending that was happening in my gut didn't stop me from continuing to believe it could still turn out okay.

My home was still there. My things were still there. The pond was still there. I had Lily. The possibility of returning to the basic outline of our lives, was still there.

For a few more days we dreamed of being okay.

We are. Okay. Mostly. It's just a different okay than what we had hoped for.

> *I found my Grandma Ethel's knitting needles. All of them.*
> *This is one of the things I was so sad to lose. I think that things like this,*
> *that someone you love has spent so many hours with for so many years,*
> *are the greatest treasures and hold the greatest magic of all.*

FINAL CHAPTER

Sometimes, when I look up from writing, I wonder, is this my life? The answer is...for now. The universe, Pele, Aila'au, all created much space for something else. What will it be? And when will it become? It will appear one day, as if fully formed overnight, but, built upon all of these other days of wondering. John Lennon said, "Life is what happens while you're busy making other plans," but I think that there are also moments within our lives when we are in between. Moments where not much living is happening at all... when so much has been erased that, for now, most of the hooks on the wall are empty, waiting for a new round of keys, and coats, and pictures.

6/16/19

Can't sleep tonight. Today I finished my first complete run through of all the essays. Hundreds of pages of essays and videos, all about my life in the jungle leading up to when our Puna floor became lava.

It's not all sadness and pain. There's humor, for sure, like my story of Poop and Maggots. And joy, like when we sat on my parking lot lanai listening to ukulele in the rain.

I wrote so much that I didn't remember what I'd written until I read it. I didn't remember what happened in between the big things. Or the exact day I found out my place was gone, along with my treasures and with my gypsy wagon. Or our last day at Pohoiki boat ramp as it was, or the day we lost Kapoho in one night, and Green Lake, and Vacationland. Then the pond. And then my Lily.

I know there are a few of you who don't understand why I'm reliving this. Those who believe life is now, not then. But time isn't linear like that, no matter what we've been told.

When trauma happens, we leave pieces of ourselves behind. Parts of our soul remain, scattered in the wreckage.

I'm not a shaman but I understand soul retrieval. I've been on shamanic descents. They altered me. Permanently. I can see and hear, and I can interpret. I can tell the stories. So, I do. I am.

We are all forever changed. We have some choice in the direction our changes take us. We can face it and decide or deny it and be led. It's the aikido of it all.

The end of the road. My road home. Someday. Photo taken 11/14/19.

ABOUT THE AUTHOR

With advanced degrees in Ecopsychology and Depth Psychology, Corey Hale has lived a unique life as both an adventurer and scholar. She is a practitioner of the human condition with expertise in the meanings and origins of fire, evolution, change, and rebirth.

Places she has called home include a sailboat in the North Pacific, an RV in the New Mexico desert, and a gypsy wagon in the Hawaiian rainforest. Corey is a thoughtful, spiritual Wander Woman whose path serves as an example of how to navigate life's most challenging experiences. She is a survivor and fierce warrior.

CPSIA information can be obtained
at www.ICGtesting.com
Printed in the USA
LVHW082343031219
639357LV00019B/1216/P